AMERICAN COUNSELING
ASSOCIATION
2461 Eisenhower Avenue, Suite 300 • Alexandria, VA 22314
www.counseling.org

American Counseling Association

2461 Eisenhower Avenue, Suite 300 • Alexandria, VA 22314

*Publisher* • Carolyn C. Baker

*Digital and Print Development Editor* • Nancy Driver

*Senior Production Manager* • Bonny E. Gaston

*Copy Editor* • Lindsey Phillips

Cover and text design by Bonny E. Gaston.

Library of Congress Cataloging-in-Publication Data

Names: Austin, Julius A., author. | Austin, Jude T., author.
Title: Surviving and thriving in your counseling program / Julius A. Austin, Jude T. Austin II.
Description: Alexandria : American Counseling Association, 2020. | Includes bibliographical references. |
Summary: "As students, we were desperate for a book that would help us prepare for and get through our counseling program. We could not find one that spoke to us. Maybe some of them were written above our heads, or perhaps some authors just could not reach two Black kids from the country. Regardless of the reason, our unsuccessful hunt for literary support sparked an idea and promise that when we could, we would write the book we needed. We believe we accomplished that goal with this book"—Provided by publisher.
Identifiers: LCCN 2019053759 | ISBN 9781556203923 (paperback)
Subjects: LCSH: Counseling—Vocational guidance. | Counseling—Study and teaching (Higher)
Classification: LCC BF636.64 .A87 2020 | DDC 158.3023—dc23
LC record available at https://lccn.loc.gov/2019053759

# Dedication

*This book is dedicated to our kids.*
*Your smiles make surviving and thriving in our counseling and doctoral programs worth it.*

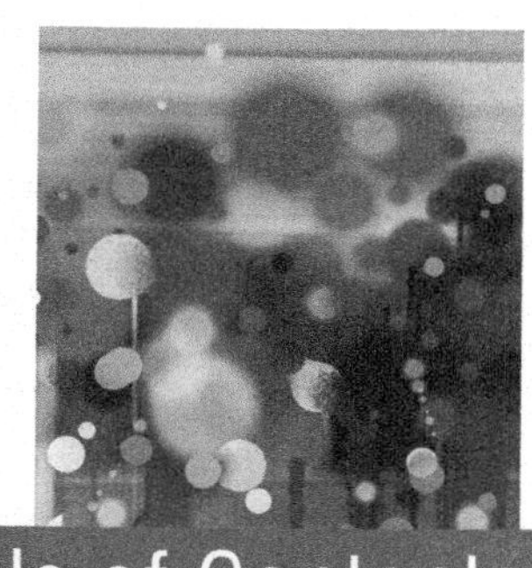

# Table of Contents

# Preface

As students, we were desperate for a book that would help us prepare for and get through our counseling program. We could not find one that spoke to us. Maybe some of them were written above our heads, or perhaps some authors just could not reach two Black kids from the country. Regardless of the reason, our unsuccessful hunt for literary support sparked an idea and promise that when we could, we would write the book we needed. We believe we accomplished that goal with this book.

You may not have been born and raised in a country town in Louisiana, but we tried our best to be mindful of the diversity of our audience when writing. In our minds, our audience is recently graduated undergraduates who applied to a graduate counseling program, got accepted, and are now in a cold sweat thinking about how they will get through the next 2–3 years. Keep reading. We may also be speaking to someone in the throes of their counseling degree who may feel like they are in a spin cycle. Your assignments are backed up, your email inbox just displays an infinity sign instead of numbers now, your relationships are strained, your self-care is a distant dream, and your next session is in 10 minutes. Keep reading.

No one can fully explain the physical, psychological, emotional, cognitive, spiritual, and relational strain students sign up for in graduate counseling. Don't get us wrong: The reward is well worth the struggle. But the struggle is real, and we were hilariously unprepared for it. If you have picked up this book because the struggle bus is currently doing donuts in your life, know that you are not alone. Keep reading. Throughout the book are chapters dedicated to some of those struggles, with down-to-earth discussions and suggestions to help you not only survive but also thrive in your counseling program.

Rather than providing a book focused on an exhaustive review of the empirical and scholarly literature on the graduate school experience, we share our experience getting through our counseling program. We have also invited contributions from a diverse group of recent graduates, new professionals, and current graduate students to share their experiences of thriving in their counseling programs. Their contributions can be read in the Voices From the Field sections.

Students can use this book the moment they decide to pursue a graduate degree in counseling. Counseling professors can also use this book as supplementary reading in undergraduate professional preparation courses as well as in graduate seminars and entry-level courses.

This book contains 10 chapters that guide you through your graduate and professional journey into counseling and offer tips for success. Chapter 1, "You Got In. Now What?," offers an introduction to graduate school. We start from the moment you get accepted. We discuss the expectations placed upon you now as a graduate counseling student. We also talk about how to prepare for this journey, both personally and professionally.

Chapter 2, "First Year," addresses some of the issues and experiences you may have during your first year. We share ways to organize your life to set you up for success before you start working with clients.

Chapter 3, "Second Year," focuses on clinical experience. We discuss not only the professional challenges you will face but also obstacles to be mindful of in your personal life. We share experiences of our first counseling session and discuss other experiences the second year brings.

Chapter 4, "Third Year," highlights the switch from graduate student to a professional counselor. We discuss closing the chapter of graduate school and share insights from our journey.

Chapter 5, "Life After Graduation" offers insight into the world you will now face as a legitimate therapist. We start from the moment you step off of the stage during graduation and discuss career plans later in life. We discuss the licensure process and the best ways to get the most out of this critical part of your counselor development.

Chapter 6, "Getting a Doctoral Degree," illustrates what you may face if you choose to continue your education by obtaining a doctoral degree. We generally discuss our experiences as well as offer other's experiences. We walk you through a step-by-step process of getting into a doctoral program.

Chapter 7, "Emotional Maturity," focuses on the intangible characteristics that define who you are as a student and counselor. Some of these characteristics cannot be taught but pulled out of you. We not only discuss these elements but also share ways you can grow into them.

Chapter 8, "Dealing With Setbacks," addresses an inevitable part of your counselor training journey: setbacks. We outline some of the most common ones and share ways to bounce back and continue to thrive in your program.

Chapter 9, "Managing Conflicts," offers insights into the potential conflicts you may face while in training. Whether those conflicts are personal or with family, colleagues, or faculty, we break them down and suggest ways to come out of those conflicts with stronger relationships.

Chapter 10, "Multicultural Considerations," highlights the cultural issues embedded in counselor training. We discuss the areas of culture you may want to familiarize yourself with and process through as you start your counselor journey.

# Acknowledgments

Writing this book was challenging and more rewarding than we could have imagined. It would not have been possible without the support of our loving and patient wives, Lindsay (married to Jude) and Megan (married to Julius). Both delivered babies around halfway into this book's writing process. While being amazing mothers, they pushed us to keep writing when we felt drained. They put blankets over us when we fell asleep at our desks. They recorded Arsenal Football Club's games and didn't tell us the score when we worked through weekends. We could go on and on. We love you both immensely.

We are eternally grateful to our parents. Their consistent love and guidance steady us and give us the security to be genuine, humble, and vulnerable in this book, with our students, and in session with clients. When people describe us in session and class, we hear them describing our parents. Our therapeutic relationships are secure because they taught us how to love. Knowing we are loved by them gave us the security to explore who we are professionally. There is no failure when you know you can always go home to mom's crawfish étouffée and dad's fried chicken and everything will be all right.

To our baby sister, Dr. Jasmine Austin, thank you for continually inspiring us as you move through academia with style and grace. Your unflinching commitment to your identity in a world that aggressively attempts to define you leaves us in awe. Thank you for driving, flying, crawling, and doing whatever you had to do to get to us when we needed you. Thanks for holding babies while we wrote and slept. Thanks for never asking us how the book is going when we call.

We also want to thank the contributors, who, without hesitation or without even being asked sometimes, stepped up for us when we needed you. Whether you reviewed the proposal, wrote a piece, reviewed the first draft, or just listened to us craft the idea for this book, we appreciate you. Thanks for always believing in us and being willing to be vulnerable with us.

Saying thank you is not enough for our counseling program faculty members at the University of Mary Hardin-Baylor, specifically Dr. Leonard, Dr. Chou, Dr. Eary, Dr. Benner, Dr. Howard, Dr. Statz, and Dr. Ballard. You have given us and our growing families a future. You have taken the lessons we have learned and our character, built by our parents and grandparents, and molded them into the therapists we are today. Thank you for seeing and training the person in us. Thank you for allowing us to be ourselves. Thank you for showing us how to serve the field and our communities with integrity. We survived and thrived in our counseling program simply because you gave us the opportunity to do so.

# About the Authors

**Julius A. Austin, PhD, LPC,** is a former collegiate and professional soccer player who earned a master of arts in clinical mental health counseling from the University of Mary Hardin-Baylor and a doctorate of philosophy in counselor education and supervision from the University of Wyoming. He is currently a clinical therapist and the coordinator for the Office of Substance Abuse and Recovery at Tulane University. In this role, he serves students struggling with substance abuse issues and works with other academic and local community resources to support students in recovery. He is also an adjunct professor at Southeastern Louisiana University and Southern University and A&M College. His research focuses on counselor development and training. He is also the coauthor of the books *Counselor Self-Care* and *The Counselor Educator's Guide: Practical In-Class Strategies and Activities.* Contact him at jaaustin16@gmail.com.

• • •

**Jude T. Austin II, PhD, LPC, LMFT-Associate, NCC, CCMHC,** is an assistant professor and clinical coordinator in the Professional Counseling Program at the University of Mary Hardin-Baylor. He is also in private practice in Temple, Texas, working with individuals, couples, and families. His research focuses on counselor education pedagogy, specifically finding ways to help counseling students develop therapeutic presence in session. He is the coauthor of the books *Counselor Self-Care* and *The Counselor Educator Handbook: Practical In-Class Strategies and Activities.* Contact him at drjudeaustin@gmail.com.

# About the Voices From the Field Writers

**Laura Capasso** is a doctoral candidate in the counselor education and supervision program at the University of Northern Colorado.

**Vanessa Dominguez, PhD,** is a therapist at Whole Journey in Chesapeake, Virginia, and an adjunct professor in the Department of Counseling and Human Services at Old Dominion University.

**Ray Eary, PhD,** is an adjunct faculty member in the professional counseling program at the University of Mary Hardin-Baylor.

**Alicia Eggleston** is a recent graduate of the marriage, family, and child counseling program at the University of Mary Hardin-Baylor.

**Gulsah Kemer, PhD,** is an associate professor in the Department of Counseling and Human Services at Old Dominion University.

**Kenya King** is a recent graduate of the marriage, family, and child counseling program at the University of Mary Hardin-Baylor.

**ShanTrail King** is a recent graduate of the marriage, family, and child counseling program at the University of Mary Hardin-Baylor.

**Kellie Kirksey, PhD,** is a holistic psychotherapist and certified rehabilitation counselor at the Cleveland Clinic Center for Integrative and Lifestyle Medicine in Lyndhurst, Ohio.

**Joel Lane, PhD,** is an associate professor and interim chair of the Counselor Education Department at Portland State University.

**Gil Lerma, PhD,** is a therapist in the CAPS for Counseling Services office at Tulane University.

**McKinley Marks** is a graduate student in the clinical mental health counseling program at the University of Louisiana at Monroe.

**Benjamin Ng** is a therapist in the CAPS for Counseling Services office at Tulane University.

**Judith Preston** is a doctoral student in the counselor education and supervision program at Old Dominion University and a therapist in private practice in Chesapeake, Virginia.

**Sarah Silva** is a doctoral candidate in the counselor education and supervision program at Walden University and a therapist in a group practice in Chicago, Illinois.

**Martha Thomas** is a graduate student in the clinical mental health counseling program at the University of Mary Hardin-Baylor.

**Areah Thompson** is a graduate student in the clinical mental health counseling program at the University of Louisiana at Monroe.

**Natasha Villegas** is an alumnus of the marriage, family, and child counseling program at the University of Mary Hardin-Baylor and a stay-at-home mom.

# You Got In. Now What?

For starters, take a deep breath and try to become increasingly aware of the sacrifices you and your family have made up to this point in your life. There may have been times where your life depended upon making one decision: turning left or right, going or not going to an event, saying no or yes, or ending or beginning a relationship. Think about your hustle—that side job you hated but needed because it helped you pay tuition or rent. Reflect upon the group projects you were required to do as an undergraduate where no one did their share, so you carried the whole team because you wanted a good grade. Be humbled by everyone in your life who contributed, in small and large ways, to you being where you are today. Know that all of those decisions and experiences have led you into this graduate counseling program for a reason.

Now, take another deep breath and read the rest of this book knowing that you have everything you need to make it through counselor training. Purchasing this book should indicate that you already seek out the support you need when you need it. You have been surviving and thriving your whole life. You will need this mentality to make it through counselor training because it is a crucible of self-determination. The training process holds, molds, and changes you forever. Everyone's journey is different, but how you process this change and the person you are becoming can either help or hinder your development as a counselor.

When we meet with students at the beginning of their journey, they want to know how to get through the counseling program with good grades and without hurting themselves or their clients. We eventually tackle that question, but first, we spend a significant amount of time focusing on helping students answer two questions: What do you want to do with your life beyond your career, and how can you use your time in the training program to prepare for that life? Answering these questions may clear the way for us to talk about the details of degree/career planning.

In this chapter, we discuss how to start the graduate program on the right foot. We share our own answers to the previous two questions. This chapter allows readers to be in the room during these early mentorship meetings as we prepare students to begin their counselor journey. It also introduces the topics we will discuss in detail throughout the book.

## The Journey Begins

You may have picked up this book after being accepted into a graduate counseling program on the first try or after several attempts. Some of you started this journey straight from your undergraduate studies, whereas others spent some time in the world before entering academia again. Before this journey, you may have had another career, raised kids, and are now spoiling grandkids thinking, "Why in the hell did I sign up for this program?" Regardless of where you were before you got here or how many times it took you to get here, congratulations. You made it.

At the beginning of our counseling journey, we wished someone would have told us that there are specific experiences in counselor training where you can thrive and others where you just need to grunt through and survive. For example, some students thrive in the classroom. These students do well on tests, take great notes, and write excellent papers. However, those same students may fear their first practice counseling session and barely survive a fishbowl activity, where the class makes a tight circle around two individuals who sit in the middle and play therapist and client. Other students are the opposite. They survive through courses and through reading notes and books over and over again to understand concepts. They struggle to write papers and need extra support from their instructors. However, these same students thrive in clinical practice situations, where they have to hold the space for a client who is expressing intense sorrow by ugly crying (the snotty-nose, shoulder-shaking, dry-heaving type of crying) for 30 minutes.

This thrive-and-survive dynamic can also parallel students' personal lives while they are going through the counseling program. You may feel like you are thriving throughout your counseling program, but your life is a dumpster fire. All students' lives are in various degrees of shambles while in counselor training. Being more aware of circumstances where you can thrive and those where you have to survive can help you adjust to the demands of counselor training. Additionally, preparing yourself and those close members of your life for the experience can help you find the balance between surviving and thriving.

## Preparing Yourself

### A Deep Assessment of Your Life

There are many things to consider when preparing yourself to begin the counseling journey. Start with a merciless assessment of your life and be honest. What are the things within your life that will cause you to suck as a counselor? Is it your laziness? Do you really not want to do the work it takes to make an impact on your clients' lives? Are you entitled? Do you have unrealistic expectations from those around you, including instructors, supervisors, and clients? Are you not great at relationships and struggle to make them work (often flitting from one broken relationship to the next thinking something will be different)? Are you attracted to drama? Do you continually stir the pot and pull others down with you in the process? Do you want everyone to like you to the point that you are willing to sacrifice yourself for this approval? Are you needy, and do you expect others to bend over backward to support you? Do you see yourself as a victim and struggle to take responsibility for the things you are responsible for in your life and relationships? Is your cup already full? Do you feel as though you already know a lot of the information presented in class, and it is your job to help the other students reach their potential? Is your life schedule hectic? Do your full-time job, kids, relationships, and other commitments not leave you enough time to reflect on yourself? Do you have past demons or past life events that trigger you today? Do you see yourself as the white knight who will swoop into your client's life and whisper words of wisdom only you can impart? Really dig deep into yourself and your life to identify these vulnerabilities. Many of these questions resonated with us, so having these experiences does not mean you cannot become a great counselor. It just means that once you become aware of these potential limitations, you have to process and work through them to become the counselor the community needs.

## Expenses

One of the more practical issues to consider when preparing to begin counseling training is the cost. How are you going to pay for counselor training? According to a *U.S. News & World Report* article, graduate school can cost between $20,000 and $80,000 (Howard, 2017). The wide distribution is related to the type of school and options to attend such as part-time, full-time, or online. Professional organizations such as the American Counseling Association (ACA; www.counseling.org), American Association for Marriage and Family Therapy (www.aamft.org), and the Council for Accreditation of Counseling and Related Educational Programs (www.cacrep.org) and honor societies such as Chi Sigma Iota (www.csi-net.org) and Psi Chi (www.psichi.org) provide scholarship opportunities. Without scholarships, the financial toll can be immense.

The expense goes beyond tuition. Here is a breakdown of what our money went toward as students beyond tuition: textbooks, professional organization dues, professional conferences, and professional clothes. Textbooks cost about $100–$250 a semester. We looked for deals on websites such as Amazon (www.amazon.com) and Chegg (www.chegg.com). We also consulted with our instructors regarding purchasing earlier versions of the texts we used. Being twins helped because we shared with each other as much as possible. Sometimes we coordinated with a cohort friend to share a book; we made a reading schedule to organize time, so we would not miss the class readings. We also checked with the library to see if they had the current or an earlier edition of the textbook.

Professional organization dues are another cost to consider when preparing to get the most out of your counselor training. Becoming a member of a professional organization may not be necessary, but it can be helpful. Often, organizations have a discounted rate for graduate students. To be fair, it was still too expensive for us as broke graduate students. The cost was definitely a month's groceries. However, there are plenty of professional benefits to joining a professional organization. As doctoral students, we joined ACA and experienced many advantages such as discounted conference rates, discounts at stores, discounts on continuing education units, and access to professional training. Joining helped us develop a counselor identity. We started to see reoccurring names in the emails and publications and dreamed that one day, we would have an impact on this field. We encourage you to deeply consider whether membership is right for you and your family.

Professional conferences are also an expense to consider. We were too broke as graduate students to attend a professional conference, but it would have been an excellent opportunity to learn. The student registration cost for the ACA conference can range from $250 to $400. There are ways to find cheaper registration fees by registering early or volunteering. You should also factor in the cost of travel, hotel, transportation, food, and other miscellaneous/unplanned expenses. There may be financial assistance opportunities for you through your counseling program. Consult your adviser or program director for ways to apply.

You may need to budget for professional clothes. You might not need to purchase professional clothes if you entered into the counseling program after already having a professional career. We did not. We came into our program straight out of our undergraduate program, and so did our holey blue jeans and old soccer T-shirts. We became bargain ninjas, shopping for clothes online and in stores using coupons and codes. We bought clothes whenever there was a sale (e.g., 50% off, holiday sales, tax-free sales), and we used gift cards. One reason for buying these clothes is because how you present yourself to clients is important. Often, a therapeutic relationship starts from the moment a client sees you, so how you present yourself can be just as crucial as any fancy technique or counseling skill in your arsenal. If you decide to buy new clothes, we suggest finding a local clothes cleaner, tailor, or seamstress and getting them tailored.

## Length of the Program

In addition to various expenses, counselor training is going to take time. Typically, it takes 3 years for someone following a standard degree plan. It may take longer if you decide to take fewer courses a semester or alter the degree plan in any way. Some students work full-time jobs in addition to being parents, spouses, or caregivers for their aging parents; these reasons would factor into a student's decision to slow down his or her process. The first year (see Chapter 2) is typically filled with coursework, but you may experience practice therapy sessions in techniques classes during your second semester. The first courses you take help introduce and orientate you to the counseling field. These classes will also introduce you to the concept of "it depends." Many decisions made in the counseling profession require a decision tree, a tool that uses a tree-like model of decisions and their possible consequences. Because some choices depend on a particular set of circumstances, you will probably hear your professors say "it depends" more than you want in this first year.

## Schedule Destroyers

### *Classes*

Prepare yourself for how much your life's schedule is going to change. For example, Jude's current program offers classes on Monday through Thursday at 2:30–5:15 p.m. and 6:00–8:50 p.m. Your decision on when to take courses will depend on your lifestyle. Students with full-time jobs or more family obligations tend to choose evening classes. Other students may not have the same family or financial demands or their schedule simply allows them to attend an earlier class. In the first semester, try a couple of different times if you are unsure. While taking those classes, we encourage you to also consider your work personality; are you a night owl, or do you need to be in bed by 7:30 p.m.? We are both night owls, so we thrived in later class times, which gave us more time in the day to get things done. Of course, we should note that because we did not have children while we were in our graduate programs, we were able to go home after class and go to bed.

### *Clinicals*

Your schedule may also change again when you start your clinical practicum or internship. In most cases, the student clinician's schedule is set by the availability of clients. If you are lucky enough to be in a counseling program with its own counseling clinic, you may have more freedom regarding when you can make yourself available for clients. We do caution students to make sure they are available for more hours a week than they need to be because clients will sometimes cancel or miss their session. If you have to seek an external practicum or internship site, you will need to dedicate a significant chunk of your week at that site. This may mean that you have to rearrange your schedule at your full-time job and at home. We encourage students to try to find a job in a place that can become a practicum or internship site so they can receive clinical hours while getting paid. We have noticed that the most successful students are those who can manage their time and energy well. Those students are also flexible and can adapt themselves to the ever-changing schedule of graduate training. In our case, just when we felt comfortable with a schedule and we felt like we were in a flow, a new semester started, and our schedule changed. Flexibility is the key to success in counselor training.

## Academic Setting

Prepare yourself to feel comfortable in your academic surroundings. This may seem trivial, but it is a necessary preparation. We have several students in our classes who have not been inside of a classroom in 20–30 years. Transitioning back into the role of a student today can be disorienting. Start by getting accustomed to the buildings and resources on campus. This could mean carving out some time before the semester starts to visit the campus and find your classroom. Pay attention to parking rules as well as availability. If you can step into the classroom, pay attention to the areas you may want to sit. If you have a laptop with a busted battery like ours, you'll need to find a seat close to an outlet. If you are attending an online program, seek out support for the online platform and call the program's learning management system specialist for a virtual walkthrough of the online platform. Seek out resources in the academic success departments on campus. Often, there are testing centers that can help students struggling with test anxiety. There may also be a writing center on campus dedicated to helping you write using the American Psychological Association style, campus technology training available to students, and library tours that will make you more aware of how to use these resources. If we could do our graduate training again, we would have taken advantage of the learning opportunities our university provided.

### Relational Changes

Prepare yourself for relationships to change. This topic could be a book all on its own. Existing relationships may suffer while you are in counselor training. This may happen because you are going through an experience that will stretch, pull, and push you to grow in ways you may not have known were possible, and your partner or friend(s) is not going through the same experience. The counselor training process teaches you to become a more self-and-other aware individual. This could mean you have become more aware of the dysfunction in your relationships and want to make changes. In addition, your connection to your family changes. Genogram assignments make you more aware of the multigenerational issues within your family and how they have affected you today. Life-span courses can give you new insight into how your parents were raised and how that influenced their development, the way they raised you, and in turn the way you raise your own children. Prepracticum and other techniques courses may cause you to process things you thought you "dealt" with, as well as teach you how to develop a healthy professional relationship. For some of you, your therapeutic relationships may be your first taste of a genuine, healthy connection. For others, learning how to be in a professional relationship, with no intention of developing a romantic relationship, may be a foreign concept.

Additionally, the child and adolescence courses influence how you relate to children, especially your own. Increased thoughts regarding the type of attachment you have with your parents and children occur. You may also begin to think about differentiation and exactly why you married or dated who you did. Diagnostic courses cause you to have a weird relationship with everyone you come into contact with. You begin to casually do a mental status exam on everyone you speak to in stores, diagnosing them and thinking about treatment plan goals. Relax, this is normal and not wrong. You will learn how to turn this off.

Inevitably, your family realizes what you are studying in school, and then come the questions, which usually start with "in your professional opinion" or "if your child client was experiencing." In case you were wondering, talking to your aunt for 3 hours about the drama between her and your grandma does not count as direct hours. (We already asked!) Other courses such as the addiction course may make you more aware of the personal struggles you have with substances. These substances may not be drugs or alcohol, but sugar or gambling. This course can also be triggering for you if you were raised in a home where alcoholism was prevalent. Each course presents an opportunity to confront the different relationships you have within your life. Learning how to have professionally intimate, healthy, and secure therapeutic relationships can also make you aware of the dysfunctional relationships in your life and how you contribute to that dysfunction.

As professors standing on the other side of the podium, we now see students' eyes bulge when they realize either they or someone in their family who they have been quietly diagnosing is in an unhealthy relationship. Or we get to see the terror when they realize precisely how they are contributing to their own dysfunctional relationships. Once you become aware of this relational process, you cannot become unaware of it. This makes you responsible for how you form and maintain relationships with others. Part of your faculty's job as gatekeepers is to assess your ability to build strong therapeutic relationships.

## Take Responsibility

This leads to our next point: Prepare yourself to take on a considerable amount of responsibility for yourself and the communities you serve. The decisions we make in session with individuals, families, couples, or children can have a profound impact on the lives of those individuals now and for future generations. Your skills, attitudes, and knowledge as a clinician can keep someone from harming themselves or others, stop the cycle of abuse, protect a child or older adult, combat racism, make the unaware aware, and get free Amazon Prime. OK, not the last one, but wouldn't that be cool? To quote the great philosopher Benjamin "Uncle Ben" Parker from the acclaimed motion picture *Spider-Man* (2002), "With great power comes great responsibility."

You also have a great responsibility, an ethical mandate even, to take care of yourself. Without adequate self-care, you run the risk of accumulating compassion fatigue and burning out. For more information on self-care and how it influences your counselor identity and development, read Gerald Corey, Michelle Muratori, Jude T. Austin II, and Julius A. Austin's *Counselor Self-Care* (2018). We see self-care as a process that can take your whole career to master. You have to work hard to build a healthy relationship with self-care.

The self-care process ebbs and flows like any other relationship. We have seasons of our career where we are masters of self-care. In these times, we find a good fit between our work demands, personal life demands, and the activities we've chosen to keep ourselves healthy. There are other times in our career, especially in graduate school and our doctoral program, where we simply did what we needed to do even if it meant staying awake for 48 hours. In those times where our self-care ebbed into nonexistence, we took care of ourselves by taking a nonjudgmental attitude. We tried not to call ourselves failures for not sticking to our self-care plan. This is easier said than done. Early into this process, we considered our self-care plan as just another thing we had to do. We thought we didn't have time to go to the gym, get 6–8 hours of sleep, or cook food for ourselves every night. We could barely keep up with all the course readings, assignments, clients, meetings, supervision, and paperwork. Not judging ourselves and appreciating the things we could do, no matter how small they were, made a big difference in how we felt about ourselves in those times where self-care became more challenging to maintain.

We will talk about specific self-care strategies for each stage of your counselor training journey throughout the book. For now, think about what self-care really means to you. Consider a realistic plan that accounts for every facet of your life. If self-care means just taking a shower every day, then be OK with that. In the words of our grandmother, "Sometimes it be like that." We hope that you feel prepared to thrive in your counseling program by the end of this book.

## This Is Not Undergrad

Now that you got into the counseling program, remember that you are no longer an undergraduate. We went straight from undergraduate to graduate school. We did not research how to adjust to graduate school or the demands of the program or what we were getting ourselves into. Brace yourselves for the biggest understatement of the decade: Graduate school is hard. As undergraduates, we felt a bit like sheep, roaming the campus trying to accumulate credits toward graduation. We bounced from one classroom to the next—stale pizza and cookies in hand—cramming for tests and barely passing. As graduate students, we were the youngest students in our class. It seemed like many of our peers had entire careers in the helping profession before getting their graduate degrees, whereas our curricula vitae did not have enough combined work experience to fill a thimble.

There was a professional feeling in class, and students came ready to work. In fact, students came to class prepared to engage with the information in a way we never did in undergraduate courses. Graduate students were also using their work experience in class to help everyone better understand the real-world application of the book's information. We saw fellow students as colleagues. The graduate program provided a ready-made professional network that would help us find an internship site and supervisors. Students who succeeded understood the connection between counseling skills and earning potential.

We realized early in our counseling program that for us to be successful, we needed to take responsibility for our education. This meant that we needed to read extra materials outside of class so that when we came to class, we could ask the questions we needed to know to be better clinicians. Graduate classes are interactive; every student is part of the educational process. To us, it also seemed like many of the graduate students, primarily the older students, focused all of their efforts on knowing as much as possible so that they could more effectively feed their families. That mentality was a significant shift for us in graduate school. Now, as faculty members, we recognize those students who are in graduate school working hard to feed their families compared to those students who are getting a graduate degree because they couldn't decide what else to do with their lives. What kind of student are you? How do you help or hinder your fellow students' educational experience?

Graduate school made us redefine how we learned. As undergraduates, we memorized information. We made flashcards and repetitiously studied them before quizzes and tests. Graduate classes seamlessly flow between theory and application. It was not enough to know the different life-span development theorists; we needed to understand how Erik Erikson's psychosocial stages of development apply to a client's life. Graduate school required flexibility in our knowledge. To achieve this, we had to build a new relationship with information. Maybe this corny metaphor will help you understand what we mean. For the record, this metaphor was more Jude's idea—unless it makes sense, then we'll both take the credit.

Imagine that you are in a forest. All of the information you need to know to get your degree are the trees/information around you. (In this metaphor, the forest probably smells like old carpet, and the sun is actually one huge fluorescent light bulb.) As undergraduates, to succeed, we felt like we needed to section off the forest into quadrants and study each quadrant systematically to know the information. This approach caused us to miss the forest for the trees. As graduate students, we could succeed by continuing to do this, but to thrive, we needed a bird's-eye view. We needed to get into a plane and fly over the forest. Doing so allowed us to see the whole forest—how it's shaped and how the trees interact with each other. Having this perspective allowed us to transition from theory to application in class and sessions. We could discuss not only specific information but also how different information related to each other and how it informed our work with clients.

To gain this perspective, we needed to understand the why of things. We needed to ask why Sigmund Freud wrote his psychodynamic approach to counseling. We needed to research this time period to understand why the theory made so much sense back then. We did the same thing with Gestalt therapy. Instead of making the same mistake everyone seems to make, equating Fritz Perls's approach to Gestalt therapy with the way the approach is supposed to be done, we studied more than Perls's work. We read his wife's perspective and other relational Gestalt therapists.

We also recognized that we learn through stories. We need the whole story of a theorist to understand his or her approach. Discovering how we learn changed our educational experience profoundly. Graduate classes transitioned from a place we went to and expected to get all of our knowledge to a space where we processed the information we learned outside of class. We wanted our instructors to educate us, but we did not place all of the responsibility of training on them.

There is also less structure in a graduate course than in an undergraduate course. As undergraduates, we found that the online components of a class were fantastic. We got updates when assignments were due.

Our faculty instructor uploaded our quiz, test, and assignment grades onto the course portal. We always knew where we stood. Group projects were more comfortable to start because our instructor selected our group members at random and organized a digital workspace for us through the course's online portal. We also had PowerPoint presentations and course timelines available to us, along with detailed instructions related to assignments.

Graduate courses, on the other hand, were an information desert called "figure it out." There was significantly less handholding; the support was evident and available, but there was no coddling. Some courses had a midterm, final, and one paper listed as the graded assignments. Those assignments had rubrics for you to figure out and follow, and most instructors did not use PowerPoints. We even had to keep up with our progress in the classes—the horror! Graduate classes offered less structure and more freedom, which was stressful for spoon-fed undergraduates like we were. It seemed like the assignments were more for our learning and growth than they were for the instructor to grade. To survive and thrive in graduate school, we had to take responsibility for our education and build a different relationship with learning.

## Expectations

From our experience, expectations are multidimensional and fluid. Expectations and the individuals holding those expectations changed at different stages of our development as counselors. As students, we had our own set of expectations for ourselves related to our performance and achievements. Our faculty members also had expectations of us. They wanted to see us mature and perform well in class and with clients. Our family expected us to do well, and they gave us the support to ensure that we did. We also experienced expectations from our culture. Being African American male graduate students in the counseling field came with obligations that we were not prepared to meet. In the following sections, we discuss the expectations of self and family and share our experiences of navigating these waters.

### Expectations of Self

It would be hard to be a graduate student without being high achieving. Higher education can inherently come with higher expectations of ourselves. One word captures the bane of our development as graduate students: perfectionism. This word has an insidious influence on counselor development, and it starts early.

You show up to your first class, and your syllabus is the only one highlighted in three colors, dog-eared, and filled with penciled questions for the instructor; you may have even found a grammatical error in the syllabus. You used an algorithm to set up a reading schedule and assignment schedule for yourself and your cohorts that would give you the highest probability of making an A. You do five complete drafts of a paper, sending each draft to your instructor for detailed feedback.

Five-page writing assignments quickly turn into 15-page papers because you just cannot fit all of the information on five pages. You have a 99% in a class, but you extend yourself to complete the extra point assignment to get the last 1%. At face value, none of these qualities are bad. But they can be dangerous for your self-esteem when paired with a feeling of never being good enough. It is that feeling that gets in your way when building a healthy relationship with who you need to be to connect with clients genuinely. This feeling causes you to put an immense amount of pressure on yourself to never make a mistake. We have seen it time and time again: Students who do this to themselves cannot handle the ambiguity of the counselor training process. Even great students, ones with 4.0 grade point averages and Graduate Record Examination (GRE) scores off the charts, may cave under pressure when they sit in front of a client or in front of their peers in a fishbowl activity, out of a fear of making a mistake. This feeling of never being good enough is made worse when the person sitting next to you in class does not have a highlighted syllabus and did not complete the extra-credit assignment, yet this person is succeeding in the class. Having a constant need for achievement, especially in a field where success is measured by the impact you have on the lives of others, can be frustrating when you are accustomed to placing your value as a person in a grade point average or test score. Our advice is to learn how to fail. We cannot tell you what this means for you, but to us, it meant finding our self-esteem in something other than how well we met our own and others' expectations. In fact, we, and this sounds weird, expected to fail. Before each session, we would give ourselves and each other permission to make mistakes. Paradoxically, taking this approach gave us freedom. The great philosopher Lorraine Austin (our mom) would say, "How can you expect to do something perfectly if you have never done it before?" We always reminded ourselves throughout our counselor training that we did not and were not supposed to know what we were doing, which made it perfectly normal to be imperfect.

## Family Expectations

Families often have expectations of you. Some of these expectations can be explicit, and some are implicit. Students often say, "My family never explicitly said they would love me less if I failed, but they always made me feel like this was the case." These expectations can have a profound influence on your development of self-esteem and self-efficacy, which are two traits you will need an abundance of if you plan to thrive in your counseling program.

To get a better understanding of the role expectations play in our development, take a moment and reflect upon your place in your family (your family of origin, your partner and children, or however you define family). Imagine you have a rope attached from your belt loop to each individual person in your family. The closer you are to an individual in your family, the tauter the rope is connecting you to that person. The rope will be looser between you and an individual to whom you feel less connected. Now think about these connections. Is your rope tauter between you and your mom but looser between you and your father? Reflect on the feeling you have regarding the tautness or looseness of the ropes. Now imagine if you were to take 10 steps forward. Because of the tightness of the ropes, some relationships may feel an immediate impact from your movement.

Let's take for example your relationship with your partner. You have both been nurturing this relationship for a while now; the rope is tight. Maybe there was a time where you felt comfortable with the tautness, but now it feels like it is harder to move. You follow your dreams and start the counseling program. You take your first class where you have to write a paper conceptualizing a difficult time in your life using three life-span developmental theories. Oh no, you have an aha moment while writing. One of the theorists explained your attachment to your parents and how that plays out in your relationships. You realize that you have the same unhealthy attachment pattern with your partner. It's 2:00 a.m. when you are writing this paper, so your partner is sleeping. Your partner has no idea that in the living room, you are making giant relational growth steps. Your partner is asleep, happy, and sees no need to change himself or herself or the relationship. Remember the rope is taut, and you both feel comfortable. Your partner wakes up and expects everything to be the way it was before, but because of this new awareness you stumbled upon, for you, everything has changed.

The counseling program continually puts you in positions where you will gain awareness of yourself in relation to others. You will start to realize that the taut ropes do not always represent healthy relationships. How can you build new relationships or modify existing ones so that the ropes are tight enough to feel secure and connected, but they are loose enough for you to grow as you need in your counselor training program?

### What Kind of Experience Do You Want?

At the beginning of our program, we decided we wanted a training experience that would influence the kind of African American men we are. We treated our counseling program as a finishing school. Our training program sharpened all of the work our parents did to instill values, dispositions, skills, and knowledge. We did not cling to who we were when we entered into the counseling program; we did not fight the change process. We welcomed this process and intentionally allowed it to shape us into something different. It was not all rainbows and Skittles. A unicorn did not float down and kiss us on our foreheads imbuing us with eloquence and grace. There were awkward times, impossibly difficult times (practically any statistics course), and times when we felt like the counseling program was precisely where we were supposed to be. We just embraced this process as much as we could. So, what kind of training experience do you want? What are some things you can do to get that training experience for yourself?

## Closing Thoughts

Our advice is to take your time during this part of your training process. There will be very few times throughout your career where you can work without much pressure because as students, all of your clinical work is supervised by supervisors who have supervisors and so on. Faculty and supervisors work together to prepare you for the field. With this many eyes and hands around to catch you when you fall, feel free to explore who you are and how you express yourself in session. Meet with faculty and ask questions. Watch your recorded sessions and watch your peers' sessions. Give feedback to peers about their clinical work and be open to receive feedback from others about your clinical work as well. Take the time to read additional books or listen to an audiobook (we count this as reading) about a theoretical approach you are interested in trying. Take your time with writing, study the APA manual, and read professional articles to learn how to write professionally. Taking your time and following these suggestions will help you strive throughout your training program.

# Chapter 2

# First Year

Welcome to the first year of your counseling program! On behalf of the dean and the rest of the faculty, I would like to welcome you aboard. Our flight time will be approximately 3 years, and we look forward to ensuring that your experience with us is challenging yet fruitful. Before we close the main cabin doors, the faculty has requested that you contact your closest family members and friends to communicate that the person they have known for quite some time is embarking on a journey that could potentially change the way they view the human experience. With the increasing demand for mental health professionals in the country, flights such as these are typically completely full. However, not everyone is a good fit for the helping profession and may decide (or have the decision made for them) to choose a different means of transportation.

At this time, please ensure that you are aware of and have been contacted by your assigned adviser and your course syllabi have been double-checked. The program requests that all social media accounts be turned off, made private, or monitored closely for any potential dual relationships with the clients we serve on campus and in the community. Remember you are now representing an entire profession with those selfies and political rants. We'd like to remind you that this is a nonjudgmental flight. Judgment is prohibited throughout the program, including group counseling, skills courses, practicum, and internship. There are several emergency exits in this program, which can be found at several points as you matriculate in the program via informal and formal assessments by faculty. Please take a moment to locate the university's graduate student handbook and program handbook for more details. Seriously, for the sake of all things sane, read the handbook. Last but not least, we should mention that turbulence is guaranteed on this journey. When turbulence arrives, please secure yourself with the resources you have available (e.g., faculty, staff, advisers, mentors, peers, family, friends) before attempting to secure others. Thank you for choosing to join our program. Now sit back, relax, and enjoy the beginning of your counseling career.

This analogy is apt because your first year in a counseling program can feel very much like a plane ride—with things that you can plan for and other things that are entirely out of your control. In this chapter, we provide specific strategies to help you make it out of your first year healthy and thriving. First, we introduce the course sequence, and then we discuss issues you may face during this year and ways to navigate these issues. We share ways we have found helpful when learning how to integrate skills, attitudes, and knowledge in both content and application courses. We also discuss the counselor identity and ways to begin developing one. In addition, we share fears that you may encounter, address frequently asked questions, suggest ways to deal with cohort drama, identify professor personality types that you may encounter, share strategies for surviving and thriving in your first mock therapy sessions, and provide options when considering how to take care of yourself during this first year.

## Preparing Yourself

Preparing yourself for your first year starts once you are accepted into the counseling program. Typically, after the application and interview process, you will be more familiar with the outline of your program. But here are some suggestions that may help as you start to prepare for your first year:

- Contact your adviser. Do not wait for him or her to contact you. If you do not know your adviser, contact the program director or the office administrator.
- Receive and review all course-specific materials (e.g., syllabi, articles, textbooks, supplementary books). Sometimes faculty will not post this information until a week before school starts. Be patient.

- Create a method of organization. It does not have to be the ultra-organized planner and whiteboard-sized calendar, but there needs to be some form of organization in place before the semester starts.

Currently, I (Julius) have just under 25 students that I am advising. My process for advising is more of a slow-burning relationship with several meetings throughout the semester for first-year students. I like to meet with my advisees 2 to 3 weeks into the semester for a brief meeting where we talk about the student's identity, reason for choosing counseling, career goals, and personal goals, and I give the student the opportunity to ask me personal questions about my family and professional questions about my career. We will also discuss the plan of study. However, most programs have a solid plan that all students will follow.

I want to establish a relationship outside of traditional advising and build a relationship based on trust, genuineness, and legitimate interest in the student's life. In that initial meeting, we briefly discuss the classes the student is taking that semester, but the primary goal is to establish rapport. Reaching out to your adviser during your first semester is crucial to building a relationship that lasts throughout your experience in the program. Here are several questions that you may want to ask your adviser in that initial meeting:

- What classes should I register for in my first and second semesters? This is particularly important if you plan to deviate from the program's plan of study.
- How do I balance work and school?
- What counseling books, outside of my course textbooks, may be beneficial for me to read?
- What courses do students typically find difficult in the program?
- Are there any possible financial aid opportunities such as scholarships or graduate assistantships?

Another essential part of the preparation process is familiarizing yourself with the course materials for the semester. Typically, each course requires particular materials for learning such as syllabi, articles, textbooks, supplementary books, online course material, and videos. Although each course has different requirements and may even have different methods of conveying information, most course syllabi tend to be similar in structure. Syllabi usually contain several important parts: (a) contact information of the professor, (b) course description, (c) course prerequisites, (d) course objectives, (e) course topics, (f) instructional methods, (g) activities or assignments, (h) evaluation and grade assignment, and (i) tentative course schedule. Although you should read the entire syllabus, pay particular attention to the sections that describe the activities, evaluation, and course schedule. In our experience, these sections generate the most student questions and tend to be the part of the syllabus that are most flexible or subject to change throughout the semester.

As you read over the syllabus, create a method of organization. Combine the tentative course schedules for all of the classes you have in your first year and create a master schedule. This master schedule should include all due dates for course activities as well as the due dates of any other course requirements. This master schedule suggestion is one of many possibilities of staying organized. No matter which method you decide, it is essential to find a technique that you can maintain with consistency throughout the semester.

## Course Sequence

This section will contain specifics about the possible course sequences you may encounter during your first year and how to ensure that your chosen courses complement the lifestyle that you want to cultivate. The landscape of courses offered within any Council for Accreditation of Counseling and Related Educational Programs–accredited counseling program creates a scenario upon which thousands of course sequence combinations are possible. Within the many different course sequence combinations, courses are typically broken down into eight categories: (a) professional counseling orientation and ethical practice, (b) social and cultural diversity, (c) human growth and development, (d) career development, (e) counseling and helping relationships, (f) group counseling and group work, (g) assessment and testing, and (h) research and program evaluation.

Within these eight categories, students typically complete courses covering the following content areas within the first year: (a) theories of counseling, (b) psychopathology (diagnosis), (c) ethics, (d) career counseling, (e) methods of counseling/beginning counseling techniques, (f) multicultural counseling, (g) human growth and development, (h)group counseling, and (i) research. In our experience, theories of counseling, psychopathology (diagnosis), and ethics courses are best clustered together in your first semester. These are some of the most pivotal courses you will take in your graduate school experience because all other courses you take afterward will refer back to a theory, diagnosis, or ethical mandate at some point.

Course sequencing determines when you will graduate. Some programs have a very structured sequence of courses for you to take. This is a benefit because it makes the program seamless for those who can follow the plan. However, this structure becomes challenging for those who cannot follow the plan because of life's many changes (e.g., having babies, getting sick, taking a semester off). In a structured plan, courses are only offered at certain times throughout the year. Faculty members would love to accommodate all student timelines, but each program has a limited amount of faculty who can teach only so many classes according to accreditation standards. Other programs, in most cases bigger programs, have the resources to hire adjuncts so that they can offer more course options. Some programs offer nearly all of the courses every semester. The benefit of open curriculums is that students can graduate on time because all of the courses are available most of the time. However, students may have very little interaction with core faculty throughout their education.

## What's Your Pace?

I know you are probably thinking, "Where is the 'graduate as soon as possible' setting on this rocket ship." Well there are several key questions that would be beneficial to examine when considering the speed at which you tackle your program:

- How many courses are required per semester to be considered a part- or full-time student?
- What's the recommended pace of your program?
- Are you allowed to take classes out of sequence?
- How is your work–life balance?
- Is there anything happening in your personal life that may prevent you from pushing the "graduate as soon as possible" button?
- Can you transfer any courses into the program from your last counseling program?
- Can you take online classes instead of in-person courses?

These are a few questions out of many possible factors that could affect the pace at which you complete your program. This is the time to be honest with yourself about what you are willing to sacrifice to complete the program on time or how you can modify your schedule.

In my experience as a faculty member, I (Julius) have had many conversations with students about their pace of progress. Within these conversations, we tackle the answers to the previous seven questions, and one of the most significant deciding factors on pacing is the question "Is there anything happening in your personal life that may prevent you from pushing the 'graduate as soon as possible' button?" This question is vital because counseling programs are time bound; faculty members painstakingly plan the classes and experiences. At the same time, you are living a life that can be unpredictable and fluid at times. Thus, the structure of the program and the unpredictability of life can be at odds. The following sections include some ideas for circumventing the obstacles created when the program and your life conflict.

### Relinquish Your Need for Control and Trust the Process

If you have not heard the phrase "trust the process," let me introduce you to the three most irritating words spoken by everyone's favorite professor. The "process" is best described as the abstract stream of time and space at which a student matriculates through the counseling program. The faculty meticulously craft this abstract stream of time to ensure that students develop into their final forms (pardon the anime expression) at the appropriate time. It also safeguards against forming a counselor identity that is not organically and genuinely you.

### Get Your Life in Order

With the phrase "get your life in order," we use the word *order* loosely because no one has their life in order. For us, this phrase does not mean having a highlighted planner or an organized whiteboard calendar. Instead, the phrase refers to collecting and arranging the broad strokes of your life for the next 3 years. Are you and your family settled in one location? When do you plan on graduating? Do you want to relocate at any time during your education or afterward? Do you expect to marry, have children, or buy a home or car at any point? Ironing out these broad strokes within your life can make balancing school and life a little easier.

### Find Your People

Family has always been a significant part of our lives, and quite honestly, family became the glue that held our lives together during graduate school. We found that our friends outside of the counseling program provided another source of balance. We also maintained relationships with mentors who made themselves available throughout our counseling program experience. This select group of about 10 family members, friends, and mentors were our people. We could call on them for support or to simply distract us when we experienced information overload from courses. Finding people you can rely on and maintaining those relationships can prove extremely valuable throughout your educational experience.

### Be Selfish. Be Decisive.

We know that being selfish is not what leads you on a path to devote much of your life and career to helping people. But sometimes being selfish with your time, whether that is time spent with family and friends or on school, helps you "recharge" and improves your mental health, which, in turn, allows you to finish complicated projects or manage stressful relationships. In addition, being decisive about the specific counseling concentration you choose, the type of clients you want to see, and the kinds of personality types you want in your life can create a streamlined path to completing your degree.

## Plan of Study

Students, along with their advisers, often develop a plan of study, which provides them with a path to achieve their professional goals and successfully progress through the program. Although we cannot tell how your specific plan of study will look, we can briefly mention the function of a plan of study, the way we create one with our students, and the benefit of maintaining yours. Jude and I began college in 2005, a time right before GPS systems were readily available to the public at large. OK, they were expensive, and we were cheap. So, during our 6-hour commute from our parents' home in southern Louisiana to our university in central Texas, we relied on an actual map. We would map out our route using computers and print a detailed list of exits, mile markers, and gas station stops the night before. But once we were on the road, we were flying blind to what was ahead of us. If construction was being done in a rural part of east Texas just across the Louisiana state line, then we would dust off the old map and get to plotting a different course. The essential function of the plan of study is similar to a road map. Most programs have a specific way each student matriculates through the program, but the plan of study is a more personalized plan specific to your educational needs.

The specificity of the plan of study is what makes cocreating the document with students so beneficial. For example, I (Julius) may be meeting with Jasmine (a pseudonym) to go over her plan of study, and she decides to take classes according to the recommended course sequence in the program handbook. No problem! Jasmine's plan of study would reflect the program handbook. However, this plan of study would not work for Lorraine (a pseudonym) who has three children in college and has decided to go back to school to fulfill her dream of being a therapist. Because she has been out of school since completing her undergraduate degree in 1986, she has decided to ease into the counseling program by taking two courses a semester. Lorraine would benefit from cocreating a plan of study with her adviser to ensure that she matriculates through the counseling program with the proper progression of classes. A significant function of the cocreated plan of study is maintenance. It is important that you work closely with your adviser to adjust your plan of study according to your lifestyle.

## Learning How to Learn

In most counseling programs, there are several types of courses: (a) content-heavy courses, (b) skills courses, and (c) practical courses. During your first year, you will typically take content-heavy courses; then, you will take skills and practical courses the following semesters. For example, if you start in the fall semester and take a full course load, then you can expect to encounter the following types of classes your first year:

Fall: Introduction to Counseling
Legal and Ethical Issues
Counseling Theories
Spring: Career Counseling
Methods of Counseling
Diversity Issues
Summer: Life Span/Human Growth and Development
Group Counseling
Research

Some programs have multiple tracks such as marriage, family, and child counseling or school counseling. In multitrack programs, this first year may look different in regard to courses. For example, the spring semester in the first year may require students to take Marriage and Family Therapy Theories instead of Career Counseling. Each program's plan of study is unique to that program.

Regardless of the course, one of the biggest obstacles is "learning how to learn" within them. We all have tried-and-true methods of learning—visual, auditory, reading/writing, and kinesthetic. Personally, we learn best through reading and writing; we must have written one million flashcards throughout our educational history. It was our way of making sure that we retained information in content-heavy courses. However, making flashcards did not work for us in our counseling program because most of the information that we were required to consume also had to be applied to real-life situations. For example, it was not enough for us to learn Erik Erikson's stages of development by memory, we also had to know how and what these stages looked like and be able to communicate that information using a case study. Suffice it to say, our heads exploded when we got our first test back in our life-span course.

From our experience in graduate counseling programs, we noticed that the information you consume will have a direct impact on how you function as a counselor. Your understanding of counseling theory, human development, or diversity issues is more important than the fact that you memorized the definitions from the text. This was a hard lesson to learn, and it sparked the transition from an undergraduate to a graduate identity. In these heavy-content courses, we still used reading and writing as our initial method of consuming the information, but we also incorporated counseling videos, podcasts, discussions with classmates and professors, and in-class demonstrations.

## Counselor Identity

You may have an existential crisis during your first year as you try to figure out where the pre–graduate school version of yourself went. This is normal. Friends and family will tell you that you have changed, and you have. Your identity as a counselor is something that you will massage and fuss over for your entire graduate experience. During your first year, you are mostly trying to maintain your own personhood while also introducing the concepts and knowledge from your classes. This push and pull between your personhood and the counselor identity creates frustration and confusion—which is a normal part of the process. In fact, it is so normal that we have begun to see two trends as students move through their first year.

- Students feel overwhelmed with three courses: theories, ethics, and diagnosis. The fear and anxiety of going through all of the theories and trying to wrap your head around seeing what fits for you is real! After reading through the *ACA Code of Ethics*, the thought of losing your license and going to jail causes nightmares. Good luck going to buy groceries after your personality disorder lecture and not secretly diagnosing everyone in the building.
- Once students become a bit more comfortable in their first year, there is a culture of "good counselor/bad counselor" that may become apparent. Students begin seeing the therapeutic process in terms of right or wrong, good counseling or lousy counseling. This can be a source of tension within cohorts.

The former trend is unavoidable and is a normal part of the counseling process. The latter trend is also a normal part of the process, but we caution you to be more open-minded with absolute definitions of "good" or "bad" counselors.

The trick to finding your personal counselor identity is to start from the inside and work your way out. Ask yourself questions such as "Who am I?" "What gives my life meaning?" "What are my views on human nature?" "How do I define healthy relationships in my life?" and "What is your personal style when relating to people?" Take your time; you do not need to have a well-thought-out answer to all of the questions. This process of self-discovery relies on you giving the appropriate time and effort to understand who you are and how you are in relationships. Now you are really doing it! You are really forming the beginning stages of counselor identity.

## The Hot Seat

Volunteering to role-play as a mock client is a built-in opportunity to explore your counselor identity. During your first year, you may not have a significant amount of chances to act as a mock client while your peers or professors demonstrate counseling skills. However, if you are lucky enough to sit in the "hot seat" and be a mock client for someone, remember these points:

- Your job is to play along so that your professor or peer can clearly demonstrate skills.
- Do not be a drill buster. Drill busters come into the mock therapy session with one million "I don't know" statements and no clear mock identity, which prevents anyone from demonstrating skills.

- Your agreement to participate as a mock client can mean contributing to a well-executed session that will enable your peer to pass the course or it could mean helping your professor to clearly demonstrate skills needed when working in real life.
- Avoid becoming a suicidal client during mock sessions unless specifically asked to do so.
- Ask your partner what particular skills he or she is trying to demonstrate in the mock session and try to adopt a client persona that is appropriate for these skills.

You may not have known going into the program that you would have to play a mock client in front of all of your peers. Areah Thompson, a graduate student in the clinical mental health counseling program at the University of Louisiana at Monroe, shares other things she wished she had known before starting her counseling program.

Voices From the Field 2.1

### Things I Wish Someone Had Told Me Before Starting My Counseling Program

***Areah Thompson***

First, we are all human. I know how invincible one can feel when they are rewarded at work. I pride myself in completing tasks efficiently. I have a competitive spirit. I have always received a "highly effective" rating at my job. I was new at this teaching thing, but I felt unstoppable. In my first year of graduate school, I soon discovered the fear of failure is my kryptonite. Having high expectations and setting goals is great. However, do understand that your expectations should be realistic and your goals can be modified. Do strive to do your absolute best, and do not stress yourself out trying to be "super student."

Second, learn to say "no." When I started school, I worked as a full-time teacher, junior class sponsor, National Math Science Initiative site coordinator, and cheer coach. I was active in my church and community. I committed a large portion of my time to friends and loved ones. I was always double- and triple-booked throughout the month. Keeping busy is one thing; stretching yourself too thin is another. Your counseling program will occupy enough of your time, so make time for self-care. Do find ways to stay social, yet don't get in the habit of saying "yes" to everyone but yourself.

Third, take your professors seriously when they tell you counselors need counseling (so budget for personal therapy appropriately). I do not like crying. I cannot stand for people to know I cried. And I absolutely hate others seeing me cry. Because I have such strong feelings about tears staining my face, I don't shed them. At least I thought I did not. My first year in my counseling program, I cried—a lot. I cried on my friend's couch when I "ran away" from home—and all of my responsibilities. I cried in the car on the phone with my professor. I cried in the car—AGAIN—on the phone with a different professor on a different day. I was embarrassed, but I felt better. I mean, my professors are all counselors, right? Had I not kept my emotions bottled for so long, I would not have spontaneously combusted. Do attend counseling sessions and find an emotionally, mentally, and physically safe outlet. Don't deny yourself the sweet release that accompanies a good counseling session.

Finally, make new friends. Your cohorts will come in all shapes, sizes, and colors. Still, you all have something in common. Whether your program is on campus or online, you will interact with these people regularly. You might as well get to know them. Trust me, you all will experience many of the same emotions throughout your first year. I did not learn this until my crying episode (and reruns). The individuals I assumed had it all together were even closer to breakdowns than I was. Do take advantage of opportunities you will have to learn from your cohorts. Do not be a loner.

As an educator, I thought preparing for graduate school would be as simple as buying cute school supplies and a new laptop. I was dead wrong. Emotional preparation is key. Writing and reciting positive affirmations daily has changed my life. I am also pretty sure writing them in my adorable weekly planner and typing them on my computer's desktop has something to do with my renewed mind-set toward school. But remembering these dos and don'ts and enjoying your current stage of life are steps in making your first year in a counseling program a lot smoother than mine. Do your best! Don't quit!

• • •

## Closing Thoughts

Graduate school is hard, and the first year can feel like a slap in the face. The first year is the beginning of your journey to get to know yourself, maybe for the first time. It is uncomfortable, awkward, and anxiety producing. Following Thompson's advice, do your best and do not quit. At the very least, talk to your adviser before you make any rash decisions. The program gets harder, but you also grow more and become accustomed to ambiguity. The next chapter focuses on the second year, the clinical year.

# Second Year

The second year presents its own set of unique challenges. Most master's students are starting the practical element of their education. This entails working in an on-campus clinic or a local clinic, managing a caseload, attending supervision, and completing more paperwork than one could ever imagine. At this time, the program requires more energy, commitment, and responsibility than most students feel prepared to handle—at least this was true for us. Students may also be receiving clinical feedback they were not expecting, realizing their limitations, and deciding if they want to continue in the program.

This chapter covers what to expect while experiencing these challenges. We also discuss ways that may help second-year students get the most out of this year. Specific topics in this section include seeing the first client, supervision, managing paperwork, the practicum experience, contemporary issues in clinical counseling, multicultural considerations during this year, and managing multiple roles.

## Practicum and Internship in Perspective

Well, you are really doing it now. You are in practicum and are seeing clients for the first time, or you have made it to internship and are getting more clients added to your caseload. Regardless of where you are in the process, you are a bona fide therapist. This section focuses on putting the practicum and internship experience into perspective, as we understand it. Broadly, these clinical experiences are a chance for you to practice the skills you have been learning and discussing in class. Part of this experience is to further develop your clinical skills. The other part of this experience is for faculty members and supervisors to see if you can handle the demands of the counseling field. So, yes, faculty and supervisors are watching you. And yes, we are talking about you all the time. And yes, everything—clinical placements, supervisors, and even who's in your practicum and internship group—is done intentionally. Faculty members want you to get the experience you need to grow into your potential. We also want to push you, sometimes to the brink of what you can handle, to make sure you will not hurt clients or yourself when things get tougher after graduation. As we mentioned before, sometimes we have students who are great in class and crumble when doing clinical work.

In our experience, practicum and internship will always ask of you more than you can give. Your spirit may be willing, but for your flesh, there are times when it will be much too much. You are asked to manage your clients, complete the paperwork, develop treatment plans, find your theoretical orientation, attend supervision, watch recordings of your sessions, watch your peers' sessions and give feedback, handle clinical crises, run groups, see couples and families, participate in clinical staff meetings, attend class, and much more. Somewhere in there you will need to find time to eat, sleep, and take care of yourself. The more clients you have, the more energy they take and the less energy you have to spread around to other obligations. Simply put, this part hurts. For many students, it's a gut punch. They struggle to catch their breath in an environment that does not have time for them to do so.

Try not to freak out. Obviously, students survive this experience. We survived it, your faculty members have, and the therapist you see also made it through this experience. So, it is possible to survive and thrive in this experience. We don't know how others did it, but we know how we did it—with perspective. We always reminded each other that we aren't supposed to know what we are doing. We are not supposed to be Carl Rogers or Fritz Perls. The benefit of going through counselor training as a twin is having these perspective chats. Before we walked out of our truck to see clients in the clinic, we sat there and said, "Let's go make some mistakes." This reminded us that we didn't know what the hell we were doing in there and that we would make mistakes. Even now, there has not been a perfect day of clinical work. With all the training, education, and letters behind our names, there are still times when we don't know what we are doing, and we still make mistakes.

## Basic Nuts and Bolts of Practicum and Internship

So far, your education probably seems segmented. Each class focuses on a different skill with seemingly unconnected pieces. You move from class to class, surviving and just trying to stay afloat. Well, practicum is where everything comes together (sort of). In practicum, you will be asked to integrate the segmented skills you have learned so far in your program and use them to build strong therapeutic relationships with clients.

So, what do you do in practicum? Generally, you see clients at your practicum site, you attend a class that is like group supervision, and then you participate in individual supervision with your site supervisor and faculty supervisor. Some programs allow doctoral students to supervise you instead of faculty members. If you can accomplish all these tasks as well as keep your schedule organized, complete all of your paperwork on time, and remain humble and open to feedback, you can survive practicum. Later in this chapter, we discuss more ways to thrive in this experience.

For now, let's shift gears to the internship experience. For those of you in internships, congratulations, you made it through practicum leaving a trail of cured clients and reunited families in your wake. You are an expert now (or maybe not). Maybe you still feel like you have no idea what you are doing. That is how we felt. You will be happy to know that typically there is not much difference between the day-to-day requirements of internship compared to practicum. You still see clients, but this time you are at an internship site, which may or may not be different from your practicum site. You will still attend classes that are structured like group supervision. You will most likely still have a faculty or doctoral-level supervisor in addition to your internship site supervisor. The most significant difference in our experience is the expectations placed upon students. Faculty don't expect to see Carl Rogers reincarnated, but we want to know that you sort of know what you are doing.

Well, we want to see an improvement in your counseling skills and other professional areas since practicum. We want to see your counseling work follow a theoretical orientation and become more focused. Mainly, we want to have confidence that you can carry your own small caseload with minimal supervision. Think of the clinical training process as one big experiment in scaffolding. First, we give you plenty of support. Then, we wean you off until we gradually kick you out of the nest and watch you plummet to your professional death, hitting all of the "ethical violation" branches on the way down. OK, it is not that dramatic, although in some unhealthy programs you may feel that this is the process. But in a healthy program, faculty members will push you to be increasingly independent. Also, in a healthy training program, you will always feel supported by your faculty and even alumni in many cases. Later in this chapter, we discuss more ways to thrive in your internship experience.

## Preparing Yourself and Family

As you probably know from reading earlier chapters in this book, preparing yourself and your significant others is an essential part of thriving in your counseling program. Entering into the clinical component of your program is no different. In fact, this is the time to have an honest conversation with your partner, family members, and friends and explain to them that you may have days where you won't have anything left in your bucket to give to them. The clinical part of our program was a time when we lost a lot of friends. We lacked time to hang out and did not have space in our lives for people that needed more than we could give.

So, with that said, what are you accurately preparing yourself for in this phase of your training? Prepare to change. Take a moment and think about who you are now. Think about your development as a person, the things you've gone through, mistakes, accomplishments, and unfinished business. Now focus on your sensitive parts—you know, the parts you're receiving counseling for and the pieces you try not to think about. Well, the common phrase "you get the clients you need" applies in this instance because it basically means you will get the clients that poke at those sensitive parts of your personal development. If you have issues with your father, there is a high likelihood that you will get a client that replicates that dynamic. If you have problems with confronting others, you will get clients who need to be confronted. We have learned that our limitations as people and clinicians quickly become our client's limitations. So, don't run away from changing. Instead, push yourself to change and grow by becoming increasingly aware of your sensitive parts. Do this by seeking supervision, starting therapy, processing with your professors, journaling, and taking advantage of those reflective papers due in your classes.

Your family won't understand what you are going through. Also, you may not be able to completely communicate your experience in a way to help them support you. I (Jude) remember my first day in practicum: My 10:00 a.m. client experienced auditory and visual hallucinations, my 11:00 a.m. client was a white supremacist court ordered to seek counseling, and my 12:00 p.m. client experienced a month-long abduction where she was repeatedly sexually assaulted. Later that day, my mom called and asked me how my first day went, and I said, "It went OK." What else was I supposed to say?

There are as many ways to prepare your family and friends as there are families. We cannot tell you exactly how to prepare your unique family to support you, but we can tell you that they cannot read your mind and they will not know exactly what you need, when you need it, unless you tell them. We have heard many clients, students, and trained professionals say, "If they really loved me, they should know what to do." No, just no. Finding a way to communicate your needs and experiences with your loved ones, without breaking your client's confidentiality, is vital. Help your family support you by figuring out what you need. Please note that there will be times where you don't know what you need. Try and make a plan for that. Sometimes calling ahead and saying you are in the mood for (insert comfort food, drink, or snack) can be all the indication your loved ones need to support you. Allow your loved ones or support system to be a part of your clinical experience in the most ethical way possible. Sit with them and run through a list of questions they can and cannot ask or the questions you cannot answer. Discuss how you are growing and what it means for the relationship. You may be growing more direct in your communication, you may be becoming less emotionally reactive, you may be harder to manipulate, or you may start setting more boundaries. Speak up; do not grow in isolation.

## Things to Consider When Finding a Site

So, you are about to finish your last techniques class: applied techniques, advanced clinical skills, or pre-practicum. You are jacked out of your mind on coffee and can't leave Walmart without making someone have an aha moment. Now would be a great time to meet with your adviser and ask to see the list of approved clinical sites. Most programs have a master list that may also identify the supervisor and location of the site. If your program does not have a master list, ask faculty and previous students and check the internet. Narrow that list down to about five or so ideal sites. The narrowing process is unique to you, but we focused on three characteristics when narrowing our list. First, we considered the distance from our home. We would have been OK driving to a site, but no more than an hour. Second, we focused on money. Because it is common for a clinical site not to pay practicum or internship students, we wanted to find a site close to home to avoid paying a lot for gas. Third, we focused on the clientele.

In Chapter 1, we mentioned that we initially ask students a question that is often difficult to answer: "What do you want to do with your life beyond your career?" The answer to that question plays a pivotal role in your decision to choose a practicum and internship site. You will take practicum, then Internship I, and then finally Internship II. Each clinical experience can get you closer to your answer if you intentionally choose your site. Sometimes the population you want to work with changes after you work with that group during your practicum or internship. For example, we have had students who came into the program wanting to work with children until they do a practicum in a children's clinic. Sometimes students want to work with children because they are afraid of working with adults, but after working with an adult during their practicum or internship, they realize they can do it. Some students complete all three clinical experiences at different sites—each with a different population—until they find the population(s) they want to work with. You do not have to specialize in one single population. For example, we have extensive clinical hours with populations struggling with addictions. However, we also have extensive clinical hours working with general diagnoses, children, couples, and families. This was by design; we chose to get a general training as opposed to a more specific clinical training experience. In many ways, because of our practicum and internship experience, we see ourselves as general practitioners.

So, what should you be looking for in a site? Well, there are a few important things to consider. Can you get the hours you need to complete the course requirements? Check your clinical handbook for the number of hours you need to complete practicum or internship. Then calculate the number of direct client hours you will need every week to meet that number; add in a little cushion for client no-shows. Make sure the site you choose can support this need. We did not mention indirect hours, which are hours you receive that are not face-to-face client hours, because no student in the history of the counseling profession has had an issue getting their indirect hours.

Also, consider if the site you choose will support you in the way you need to be supported. Please note that we said *need,* not *want,* to be supported. When you visit or call, be more aware of how clinicians and staff treated you. Did you get a good vibe? Can you see yourself working under the supervision of the clinicians there? Remember you are interviewing the clinical site just as much as they are interviewing you. We went into practicum and internship knowing we had some skills; well, we could sit in the counselor's seat without vomiting on the clients. But we knew we needed more support writing treatment notes, managing cases, and developing a theoretical orientation. We also knew we did not, and still don't, want to be micromanaged. We work best when we know the expectations and are given space to meet and exceed those expectations. You will get support and feedback until your head explodes while in practicum and internship. How do you like to receive feedback? I (Jude) thought I loved my feedback served cold with a side of honesty, until a supervisor served up an ice-cold plate and one teardrop rolled down my face. Now I prefer balanced feedback; tell me what I am doing well and how I can grow.

Will you grow? This is the big question because growth is what this whole part of your training is about. Honestly, think about your experience so far. If you are going into practicum, think about your struggles in classes and practice sessions. If you are going into internship, think about your experience in sessions and in your practicum clinic. Think about what you know in your heart to be your growth areas—the ones you want your supervisor to skip over when he or she is watching your recorded session. Do you struggle to keep appropriate boundaries? How is your paperwork? Do you find it hard to do in-depth work with your clients? Do you feel totally overwhelmed and unsure you should even continue in the program? Your supervisor can help you with all of these types of questions. Look for a site that can help you grow in those areas. Try to picture yourself at the end of this clinical journey, then intentionally craft your clinical training experiences to mirror that.

You may be at a program that does not value clinical training as much as you need. Maybe that program values publications by faculty instead of producing quality clinicians. Try not to allow that to hinder your development. Take your education into your own hands. Reach out to clinicians in the area and ask for mentorship. Seek advice from your faculty members; well—that one faculty member that actually answers his or her emails. Join a professional organization such as the American Counseling Association and take advantage of their webinars and trainings. Finally, read everything! Devour books on the topics you want to know more about. Trust us, we know how boring some of the writers are in this field. Do not give up; find the authors that speak to you and stick with them.

Will you get paid? The ultimate dream for us as students and our students now is to find a paid clinical site; it's like the Holy Grail. Unfortunately, in most cases, practicum and internship sites do not offer payment. This presents a common struggle for students as they consider whether or not to quit paying jobs to fulfill the practicum requirements. We do not have the answer for you. We do know that students who are intentional and organized have a better chance of finding a situation that works for them and their families.

The next question students usually ask after finding out that their practicum or internship site may not pay them is, "Can I turn my existing, paying job into a practicum or internship site?" The short answer is maybe. Here are some very basic elements you need in a clinical site: clients you see face-to-face, a licensed supervisor, and a way for your faculty or doctoral supervisor to view your clinical work. There may be more needed as these requirements change from program to program. If you are at a site where those basic elements exist, then there is a chance. Consult with your supervisor and discuss ways to get that site approved as a practicum or internship site. It usually involves a site visit and signing of a site agreement form. Our advice would be to start this process well before you start your practicum or internship experience. This would increase the chances of the site being approved by the time you are ready to use it. In the following section, McKinley Marks, a graduate student in the clinical mental health counseling program at the University of Louisiana at Monroe, shares her experience in practicum and securing a site.

Voices From the Field 3.1

## Considerations Regarding Practicum Site

***McKinley Marks***

Going into my practicum experience, I had no idea what to expect or hope for. What was going to be expected from me? How much freedom, or lack thereof, would I be given to share my input? Quite frankly, I felt underprepared and overwhelmed simply thinking about the upcoming semester. Two weeks prior to classes starting, my site unexpectedly fell through, and I was left with no backup plan. (Lesson learned: Always have a backup plan.) I started making panicked phone calls and thankfully uncovered connections through a previous employer. Sometimes it truly is all about who you know. Is this fair? Absolutely not! Is it the reality of today's society? Unfortunately, yes. In my case, this worked out in my favor. After 2 intense weeks of anxiety, and several frantic emails back and forth with my practicum professor (the fabulous and lifesaving Dr. Julius Austin), I found myself at an acute inpatient psychiatric hospital. This site and client population were not exactly what I had in mind for my first clinical experience; however, I was so grateful for the last-minute opportunity.

Because of my late start, all of the legal paperwork (the dreaded memorandum of understanding) took a few months to come through. I officially started observing at my site in late October; I was months behind my peers. After the required observation period, I was expected to colead and facilitate psychotherapy group sessions. I had a "thrown to the wolves" feeling in my gut, and once again I was very overwhelmed. I wish that I could tell you that I crushed it and said all of the right (very smart) things. But I honestly can't remember a single thing that I said. Maybe I blacked out. Or maybe I let my nerves get the best of me. Either way, I must have done just fine because my supervisor asked me to lead another group the following day. Here's my point, you are going to be nervous and very uncomfortable. It's OK to feel like you have no clue what you are doing. Trust your instincts and remember that you have worked very hard for this moment.

In retrospect, I believe that it is important not to go into practicum or internship with rigid, preconceived ideas about how your experience will go. My experience was the complete (at least 99%) opposite of how I had imagined it. For example, I learned a ton at my site over the course of a single semester. I learned about diagnosis, short-term treatment planning, and medication management. Your experience at your site, whether good or bad, is a tool for your professional development. You have the chance to learn where your passion lies within this profession or you may determine that certain environments/populations are not the best fit for you. At the end of the day, you will be able to say that you gave it a try. Perhaps my greatest insight was that my professional aspirations do not align with a short-term treatment setting. Use this time to get your foot in the door for future hiring opportunities. Network with anyone who comes to your site; introduce yourself and express that you are eager to learn.

• • •

What stood out to us in Marks's experience was the idea that your practicum site is a tool for professional development. Choosing a site based on the type of experience you could have is important. In addition to this choice, students may get more out of the experience if they enter into it with an open mind. Marks suggested that students check their expectations regarding the clinical experience they will receive at their practicum or internship site. This emotional check before entering into a site can help you avoid being disappointed. It can also provide you with an opportunity to learn something unexpected, such as how not to give feedback or the sort of supervisor you do not want to be. Monitoring expectations can help you see the entire experience as a chance to learn something new.

Speaking of learning something new, Dr. Ray Eary, an adjunct faculty member in the professional counseling program at the University of Mary Hardin-Baylor as well as our mentor, has witnessed many students' first sessions. He watched our first sessions and our last as graduate students. Thus, we thought it fitting that he supports you as you begin your clinical journey. In the following section, he shares his insights and advice on how to slow down the process and avoid feeling overwhelmed.

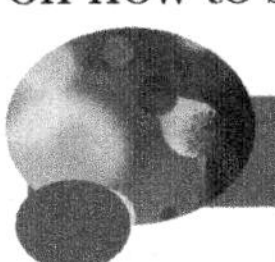

## Voices From the Field 3.2

### Surviving Your First Session

***Ray Eary***

So, it's that time. The time that you have been both dreading and looking forward to. Time to see your first genuine client. No more role-playing and simulations. No more listening to Larry (one of your cohorts) cry about how his dad ran over his bicycle when he was 10 and he lost his sense of independence or Susan telling you for the umpteenth time about her deep dark secrets of cheating while playing Words with Friends with best friends who moved to Europe. Yep, it's showtime! This is where all the preparation and practice come to fruition. Your client's appointment is Thursday afternoon at 2:00 p.m. and you already know some basic information about her, but for some odd reason, even this little bit of information is unsettling, and it's only Monday! So, let's take a look at some of the things you might want to do in this short week.

- Breathe. It is very hard to hold your breath for 4 days. Be aware of your breathing and practice the techniques that you have been taught to do with your future clients. Breathing is always a good idea but is especially important when under stress and anxiety.

- Talk to your cohort because they are probably feeling the same things. OK, maybe not Larry or Susan, but talk to the one or ones that you are close to and trust. Again, as you have been taught, practice the techniques and skills that you will soon be using with clients on yourself.
- Closely monitor your self-talk. It is not uncommon at all for the thoughts that fuel our anxiety to run away from us.

What is the worst thing that could happen? No, not that! In over 40 years of counseling, I have never had a client die during the session. I'm sure it probably has happened somewhere, but the likelihood is very slim. What if the client doesn't like you? Come on, everybody likes you, at least a little bit. Clients come to counseling because they have a problem and hope that you can help them with it. They are not coming here looking for an enemy or someone to get mad at.

What if nobody says anything? Well, you might want to start a conversation. This is, after all, an intake. You have certain things that you have to do and questions that you have to ask. This normally stimulates conversations and sharing. Remember the session is only 50 minutes long and dealing with all the paperwork is going to take a while.

What if I say something wrong? I guess we would have to define *wrong* here. If we are talking about some kind of counseling technique going awry, then welcome to the club. We all do that. Even after 40 years of counseling experience, I can and do make mistakes. The client probably does not know cognitive behavior therapy from eye movement desensitization and reprocessing and does not really care. They are interested in being heard and more importantly understood. Because this is your first session and an intake to boot, you are probably not going to be using a lot of theory-based intervention strategies. So, just be you. You did not get to be as old as you are and almost finished with a demanding graduate curriculum by being naive or closed off.

OK, Tuesday finally comes, and you are feeling better. You have heeded the above recommendations and now understand that you are not alone. Remember you were taught to normalize the client's behaviors and feelings, so you can also normalize your anxiety and negative self-talk with your peers. You are all in the same boat.

This may be a good time to refresh yourself with the intake forms, confidentiality exceptions, fees, and so on. Remember anxiety is about the future; once you make yourself busy, it starts to go away. If you have the time, maybe a short practice session with one of your peers who is ahead of you in the program might be in order. They have already been through it and can give support and positive feedback.

Wednesday is like Christmas Eve. It's the day before the big event. In this case, you already know what your present will be—the beginning of a lifelong career in the helping fields. It's too late to cram. This is the best time to relax and maybe enjoy watching a colleague perform his or her first session. It will be reassuring to see that your colleague does better than expected. It may give you even more confidence in your abilities ahead of your session. This is a special time you will always remember, so take time to enjoy the experience.

Thursday arrives and you jump out of bed with eager anticipation. OK, so maybe you don't "jump" out of bed, but you do drag out of bed, eat a good breakfast, run some errands, and then head to the counseling center. Whoa! You didn't know most of the cohort was going to be there to watch. Actually, there are only your four closest colleagues and they are here to support you. The clinical supervisor is smiling and reassuring. You argue with yourself, hoping the client doesn't show but also wanting him or her to show. Your client is there and on time! You breathe, flash a fake smile to your friends like you are going in to see the principal for some infraction, and then walk into your future. You greet your client and suddenly the anxiety goes away and is replaced with positive motivation. The session goes so much better than anticipated and you are now a veteran counselor!

Remember your client will forgive all your counseling sins if they think you care!

• • •

Dr. Eary reminds us that we are not supposed to feel like we know what we are doing in our first session. Although we have the training and support, we are supposed to feel anxious. He also expresses that it is OK to not be OK. Settle into that statement. Do not run away from your anxiety or try any excessive techniques to conquer your anxiety. Instead, make the anxiety your best friend, breathe into it, and walk into session fully aware of, and acknowledging, your anxiety.

As we mentioned, Dr. Eary watched our first sessions live. When we walked back into the supervision room after our first sessions, Dr. Eary was sitting in what we call his "captain's chair," waiting to process. We were ready to hear all of the negative things we did and how he and everyone else could tell that therapy just was not our thing and we should quit now before we get too deep into the program. Instead, the first thing he asked us is the first thing we ask our students today: "What did you like about your session?" It is a simple question, but such an important one. Of course, we said, "Nothing." He said, "We'll keep showing up until you find something you like."

We slowly forgot about the number of reflections and open-ended questions and how many feeling words we were able to rattle off in session. Instead, we focused on the subtle personal aspects of our sessions that made us a comfort to others. Soon after our first sessions, we said things such as "I like how patient I was with myself as I stumbled through the paperwork," "I am starting to criticize myself less," or "I love how we laughed when I could not remember his name." You will be nervous, and you will make mistakes for the rest of your career. The students that thrive in the practicum experience are those who are humble enough to own their mistakes and courageous enough to acknowledge them in session and supervision.

## Raising Your Game

What separates a practicum student from an internship student? We like to think of it like this: In practicum, you should not and probably will not be left alone in the clinic. However, in internship, your faculty and colleagues want to be sure that the clinic won't burn down if your supervisor leaves you alone in the clinic for an hour while they grab lunch. In other words, internship focuses on independent application of skills and knowledge in the clinical setting.

You may be wondering what independence looks like in a clinical setting. From our perspective, a typical day in the life of an independent intern looks something like this: You arrive in the clinic by 7:30 a.m.; your first client is at 8:00 a.m. You get to your office, set your things down, say good morning to the other clinicians in the clinic, and turn on your computer. You log into a client management system such as Titanium and see that you have a couple of new client intake sessions to meet in addition to your regularly scheduled sessions. It is 8:00 a.m.; your regularly scheduled client is here. You use the theoretical orientation that best fits who you are as a person and counselor. The session goes well, and you finish your SOAP (subjective, objective, assessment, and plan) note before your next session. You follow this process until lunch, and then you prepare for the new intake. The new intake shows up, and you build a solid relationship. It is so strong that the client reveals his or her plan to harm himself or herself. You begin the crisis protocol, stepping out when appropriate to bring your supervisor into the process. You and your supervisor work together to get the client the help that he or she needs. It is 1:50 p.m. Your intake session is over, and you take the 10 minutes between your 1:00 p.m. and 2:00 p.m. clients to finish the treatment notes. You see your 2:00 p.m. client and skillfully create a safety plan with a client who has shared passive suicidal ideation. Your day is done. You have finished your notes and called all the clients who missed their sessions.

We hope you noticed that being independent does not mean doing everything by yourself and never needing support. It means that you feel comfortable to use your professional discretion regarding when to seek support and when to rely on your skills. Your clinic colleagues can count on you to be a working member of the clinic—no drama or issues, just hard work. In addition to discretion, raising your game means to elevate who you are professionally and how you work. Push yourself beyond just reflecting content and feeling in session. We like to call this process "reading the matrix" because you start to see more than what the client is telling you during a session. In a 5-minute conversation with clients, you are hearing their words and listening for how they move when speaking and how their culture, gender, or sexual orientation influence those words. You are also listening to how society and their family, past, trauma, and addictions are influencing everything they are saying. It feels like you are listening to nothing and everything at the same time. The therapeutic process becomes a tangible thing you can see and feel in the therapy room.

## Therapeutic Process

So, at this point in your education, you will probably hear the phrase "trust the process." If you are like us, you might respond with "Yeah, I know," but in your head, you are thinking, "What the hell does that mean?" We can only share with you what it means to us now, at this stage in our development. We imagine that this phrase has one of those annoying shifting meanings that changes as you grow. Anyway, do you remember that tangible thing you can see and feel in the therapy room—the process? Well, there is a lot of growing you have to do to get to that feeling of reading the matrix in session. You may not even get to it by the time you graduate. We hope our discussion of the therapeutic process in this section can get you started in the right direction. We begin with an important question: What is good therapy?

You know those moments where you make yourself a cup of coffee, and it's something about the sugar-to-cream ratio that just makes that cup special. Or you know that feeling you get right before it's about to rain like there is just something in the air. Or that feeling of stillness and quietness you get when you walk outside right after it has snowed. These feelings share a multisensory experience that we think exists in a good therapy session. In those sessions, you are more than just a technician doing prescribed techniques found in some manual. Your clients experience your sessions with all of their senses and feel a genuine connection to you.

To create this climate in session, you have to push yourself to experience your sessions with all of your own senses. This way of working with clients is called being therapeutically present. Do not mistake being therapeutically present in session with being present. You will also hear the phrase "be more present" a lot. When counselors said this phrase, we wondered what they meant exactly. Were they referring to not being distracted, to being physically present in the chair, or to something else? We prefer the term *therapeutic presence* because it is more than just focused sitting and listening, which is also important. Being therapeutically present in session is a process, a way of doing therapy as opposed to a way of being in therapy.

The more seasoning or experience you gain in therapeutic relationships, the more therapeutically present you can be in session. Right now, at this point in your training, try to see therapeutic presence as an increased awareness of yourself, the client, and the therapeutic relationship. Now once you have increased your awareness, you can use it to act in a way that is therapeutic for your client from moment to moment. For example, if the client is anxious, then you become anxious, and the anxiety turns into fear, and you can feel it in the relationship. You start to feel like things are out of control within yourself now. Instead of running away from those feelings by talking about something totally unrelated to the anxiety in the room (which is not being therapeutically present), open yourself up to the feelings and acknowledge them. Focus on the feelings within yourself, the ones you recognize in the client, and how yours and the client's feelings interact with one another within the relationship. Then, reflect out loud in the moment how you think the process you just experienced with the client relates to their presenting problem.

The more you practice being aware of yourself and the client within session, the stronger your therapeutic presence will be. Research shows that when clients experience their counselor as being therapeutically present, they have more positive treatment outcomes. Being therapeutically present in session is like building a muscle. The more you use your awareness of yourself, the client, and the therapeutic relationship to act in a way that is therapeutic and healing, the stronger that muscle will become. As you continue to grow, you will be able to bring more of yourself into the session. According to Geller (2017), advanced clinicians experience being therapeutically present with clients as bringing all of who they are in session on multiple levels: physical, emotional, psychological, spiritual, and relational.

In case all of this talk of being therapeutically present with your clients on multiple levels is flying over your head, we will bring the therapeutic process down to earth. When you sit down with a client, try to think of the process like a layover in an airport. You are already at your next gate; you've eaten and gone to the bathroom. There is nowhere for you to be or go at the moment. Just sit and listen; there is no rush. That is what being therapeutically present in session might look like for you—just sitting, looking, and listening with no rush.

As graduate students, we were taught the Carkhuff model (1967) of counseling (an old-school way of looking at the therapeutic process). This model provides us with a loose structure to follow in session, and the structure gently guides our process. A couple of years ago, a student described our process as the "made bed" method. We know it sounds weird, but just go with us here. Imagine that the mattress is the therapeutic process. The first thing on the mattress is a fitted sheet—that weird scrunchy one that's impossible to fold. In this analogy, the fitted sheet hugs the mattress (the therapeutic process) and is your natural presence—how you naturally influence those around you to be closer or more distant from you with your body language, voice, and other characteristics. The second layer, the top sheet, is the Carkhuff model. This model provides structure, without hampering creativity. This model is our safety net, and we fall back on it when we get overwhelmed in session. The last thing on the bed is a comforter, which is your theoretical orientation. Your theoretical orientation drapes over your personal therapeutic characteristics and the Carkhuff model, and it directs your focus in therapy. Because of it, you may choose to focus on the client's irrational beliefs, unfinished business, feedback loops, differentiation, earliest memories, or solutions. When the layers work well, they support one another. As you go through the program, you will be forced to know the personal characteristics that help and hinder the therapeutic relationship. Additionally, you may not be taught the Carkhuff model, but you will be taught a model. The piece of the therapeutic process that we struggled with was finding our theoretical orientation.

## Theoretical Orientation

Essentially, a theoretical orientation is the counseling theory you will choose to use when working with clients. There are far more counseling approaches than you will find in your theory textbooks. Your theoretical orientation is an essential part of your clinical work. This orientation is how we conceptualize clients' background and their presenting problems. When you are introduced to these theories in your theories course, the anxiety and confusion will begin. You will feel overwhelmed by the options and probably confused because it can seem like all of the theorists say the same thing, but they use different words.

As much as we wish it were so, unfortunately, the process of choosing your theoretical orientation doesn't resemble the moment when the wand chooses the wizard in *Harry Potter*. You have to work and figure out your orientation for yourself. Unfortunately, not all counseling programs teach students how to be introspective. As educators, we hope to push students to get to know themselves so intimately that their theory becomes increasingly evident as they progress through the program. The more you build increasing amounts of self-awareness, the greater the chance you have for your orientation to reveal itself. Get out of your own way!

You may feel like everyone and their grandma is asking you about your theoretical orientation when you start seeing clients. The common answers students give are person-centered therapy, cognitive behavior therapy, or the dreaded "I'm eclectic." The latter response is dreaded because we know what students are really saying when they say eclectic: "I have no idea what theory to use, so I plan to make a game-day decision in session and shift from theory to theory with every client." This is not ideal, but we cannot judge anyone because when people asked about our theoretical orientation as graduate students, we said eclectic. It was so hard for us to be congruent in session. We felt like we were playing therapists instead of being ourselves in therapy.

The only truly eclectic clinicians we have seen practice are Dr. Gerald Corey and Dr. Ed Neukrug. They have been doing clinical work since well before we were born. They both know the theories so well that they are able to integrate them and use them seamlessly from moment to moment in session. It is far better to be philosophically pure and theoretically eclectic from our perspective. For example, if you were existential, you could use techniques from all theories but infuse the existential philosophy and treatment goals throughout your work. All of your techniques would have an existential flavor. Also, remember that all of the theorists were old, White men. If you are a young Indian woman, you may look at these theories and think, "I do not see myself in these theories." This is why it is important for you to make it *your* theoretical orientation.

We felt like we made more progress with our theoretical orientations when, instead of trying to fit ourselves into a theoretical orientation, we tried to better understand what caused clients issues. We then chose theories that had the technical language to explain our personal understanding. We tried out a few theories and chose a couple of them to try in session for a week or two until we found the one that felt less forced. We eventually landed on an approach that fit our personalities, past, life lessons, family lessons, values, and cultural background. There was a time, in Internship I, where things started to click in session. We started to "read the matrix."

OK, in summary, do you really need to choose and apply a theoretical orientation by the time you graduate? No, but it wouldn't hurt. And no, we cannot reach through this book and identify your theoretical orientation; well we could, but we are choosing not to do so. And also, stop asking your faculty members to tell you what theoretical orientation they think you are. That is cheating. We all had to make many mistakes to find ours, and now it's your turn.

## Staying Organized

Before starting clinical work, staying organized was helpful. It was pleasant to have your class notes and papers organized into folders and backed up on an external hard drive. However, now that you are in the clinical part of your program, staying organized will save your career. It is more than helpful; it is your life. Imagine needing only 1 direct hour to compete the requirements to graduate but having no record of you obtaining that hour. Or imagine that the state board will count a certain number of direct or supervision hours toward licensure, but you miscounted your hours and have to pay for another quarter of supervision. Yes, your university probably has backup copies of your documents. But what if there is a fire or natural disaster, or an intern deletes the data? Do not rely on other people to maintain your records.

During this time in your training, you will be introduced to the more cherished element of the counseling profession—paperwork. In case you cannot catch our sarcasm, we will be frank: Paperwork sucks, but you have to do it. Keep in mind that every program is different and will require you to have several different forms and documents to complete. However, your hours log is by far one of the most important pieces of documentation you need in practicum, internship, and beyond. We still have our hours log just in case someone tries to take our degree away.

Here are a few ways we have been able to stay organized during the clinical part of our program:

- Develop a way to keep track of your hours. You could use an app or pencil and paper. We used an Excel spreadsheet where we recorded the date and the kind of hours (indirect or direct). Your counseling program will most likely have some way for you to keep track of those hours. However, as we mentioned previously, it is always smart to have your own personal records.
- Record your hours at the end of each day. Do not wait until the end of the month.
- Keep a detailed calendar. Some students prefer a book or notepad calendar. We preferred to use the calendar app on our phones because it synced on all of our devices. We were able to set up alerts to remind us of meetings, assignment due dates, gatherings, and social events. Remember those direct hours are like gold; please do not miss a session and jeopardize your future because you forgot to record it.
- Buy a three-ringed binder and hole puncher with plastic separators. Keep all of your loose papers from class, supervision, consultations, presentations, meetings, and so on. We made binders like that, and they are sitting in our offices today.
- Create blank templates for session notes, contact notes, treatment plans, intake summaries, and all other repetitive documentation you create every day. You will have to personalize these for each client but having something started will save time.
- If your clinical site does not use a paperless system, you will be printing and signing an obnoxious number of documents.

Your clients will also have to sign informed consent and other documents. Find a writing utensil organizer like those children's coloring boxes and place what you need in there. Do not put yourself in a position where you are scrambling for something to write with all day.

- Answer your emails! It's time to grow up now. Unread emails can ruin your career.
- Organize your emails into folders. Do not have all of your emails sitting in one big inbox. Read them, flag them if you can't respond at that moment, and then place them in a labeled folder after you have responded.
- Find a document storage system, preferably a digital system such as iCloud, Google Drive, or Dropbox. We have seen the terror in a students' eyes when they realize they left their flash drives in a library computer one too many times.
- Organize your documents into labeled folders on your computer and storage systems. Do not have an unorganized mess of randomly named Word documents mixed with PDFs and Excel documents. If you misplace things, it could cost you your career.

## Being in Supervision

We discuss the topic of supervision in greater depth in Chapter 5, but we briefly touch on it in this section. First, let's define supervision. Essentially, you will meet with more experienced clinicians to discuss all facets of your clinical work. These meetings will occur every week from the moment you start practicum until graduation. Some programs have live or recorded videos of your sessions. Other programs may not have the capacity to view recorded sessions every time you meet with your supervisor and may require you to record your own sessions. In supervision, you will review your sessions, look over your paperwork, and conceptualize your cases. Yes, you will review the good, the bad, and the ugly. However, the whole point of supervision is to ensure that you are providing the best level of care for your clients, not to denigrate you. If you feel denigrated, speak up. Do not sit there and allow your self-esteem to be diminished one supervision session at a time. Your supervisor will also evaluate your work. Every program has its own unique way of evaluating students, so be sure to know this evaluation process and have questions for your supervisor.

If you are like us, you will want to impress your supervisor. We tried our best to hide mistakes if at all possible. Do not do this! This is the one time in your career where you can make clinical mistakes (within reason) and suffer very few long-lasting consequences. Go into session and push yourself to do life-changing therapy with clients. Use this time to sharpen your clinical note-taking and documentation skills. Trust that your supervisor will guide you into reaching your potential.

The challenge with supervision in practicum and internship is receiving mixed messages. You will probably have two supervisors: a site supervisor and a faculty or doctoral student supervisor. Sometimes those supervisors will want you to do two different things in session. For example, one supervisor may want you to focus on the client's past, whereas the other one may ask you to ignore the client's past. How do you make them both happy? We do not know the answer to this question, but we have a possible solution. You could organize a meeting with both supervisors to discuss how to proceed with the identified client. Remember this is your clinical training, so take responsibility over your experience.

## Closing Thoughts

Your job as a graduate student is to grow. Mistakes inherently come with this process. Finding our flow involved starting each day accepting and recovering from this part of the process. Clinical work is a game of recovery. For example, you spelled a word wrong and your supervisor wants you to rewrite your note. Recover. You walk into session with a perfect plan to use this fancy technique you read about in a book, but your client walked into session in crisis. Recover. You get a bad evaluation from your supervisor because you struggle to do in-depth work with clients. Recover. When a client shares his or her story, you have an aha moment and realize you too are unhappy in your marriage. Recover. The list goes on and on as well as the process. We eventually surrendered to the ebb and flow of this process, and before we knew it, we had found a rhythm. Try to settle into your process because it will be over before you know it. In the next chapter, we discuss the third and final year of your program, the beginning of the end.

# Chapter 4

# Third Year

Welcome to your third year! Most counseling programs are 2.5–3 years but can take longer depending on your degree plan. We will be writing this chapter as if you will be graduating after your third year, but we also hope to provide beneficial information to those of you who are taking a slower pace. The final year of your counseling program can potentially be the last year of your educational career. While this is an exciting time, it can also be daunting. Feelings of inadequacy creep in more than ever when you are leaving the nest. During this year, you may be terminating with clients and your internship site. Your cohort, with whom you have grown close, is preparing to separate and start new jobs. You are closing a significant chapter in your life and preparing to turn the page and start another. To help with this process, this chapter includes shared experiences regarding what to expect in this year of the graduate program. As in the previous chapters, we focus on the personal and professional challenges and growth opportunities presented in this year.

Before we discuss ways to prepare yourself for the final year, Benjamin Ng, a therapist in the CAPS for Counseling Services office at Tulane University, shares a clinical experience from after his master's degree. We hope his experience puts the learning process, the therapeutic process, and what it means to be a good therapist into perspective.

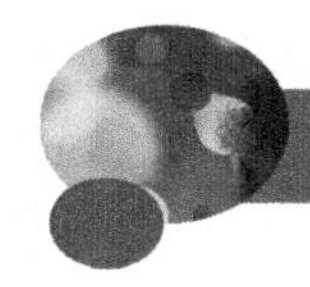

## Voices From the Field 4.1

### Best Counselor Fantasy

***Benjamin Ng***

I would like to ask you to put down the cape. To be completely frank and vulnerable with you, I had this fantasy of being "the best counselor." I wanted every session to be an explosive epiphanic moment, to the point that my supervisors, coworkers, and even clients would say, "Wow, you're a brilliant counselor!" This fantasy was somewhat self-serving to my ego, but it also housed this deep desire to want to "save the world" and to rid people of their emotional suffering. I wanted to be the last counselor every client worked with. It's incredibly validating when a client says, "I've had so many counselors, but none of them were as good as you!"

But this fantasy is a fallacy. It's a dangerous path to walk down. It has a high potential to sway you from the theoretical model you "married" for the sake of aiding the client. It can bring an insidious, conceited energy into the room that clients can pick up on—either averting them away from you or drawing them toward you to manipulate you. Either option leads to client disingenuity. There is no doubt that you have good intentions—you are in the helping profession after all—but it places a barrier in front of authentic connection. It has a flavor that inadvertently perpetuates an "us–them" mentality. This is different from being confident and competent in what you do.

The setting in which the clients are receiving services and their current stage of change are important here. When I was working at an inpatient addictions facility, I had to remind myself often that the primary work I was doing wasn't meant to resolve all that my clients came in with. It was purely to help clients achieve sobriety in the moment, allowing them the ability to thoughtfully access all that they needed to work on. The unravelling of their psyche, although necessary for long-term recovery, was not my job—that was work for their ongoing counseling sessions with a community therapist. It was a slight grieving process for me, especially with my psychodynamic inclinations. You can plant seeds and water them, but you can't be the sun as well.

A year into my work as a provisional licensed professional counselor at an outpatient addictions facility, I met with a client with whom I'd only had a handful of individual sessions. The client was about to transition out of my care and into the care of a counselor in the community. This particular client struggled not only with substance use but also with sex addiction, and the client disclosed having over 500 sexual partners throughout his or her lifetime. The client professed statements such as, "No one will ever love me! I'm useless. I'm broken beyond repair!" I did the standard maintaining eye contact, slight head nodding, and other emblematic active listening skills. However, it was met with a facial scowl and the following impetuous proclamation: "Why the f— are you drinking out of that cup?" I was aghast and replied, "What?" The client responded, "Why the f— are you drinking out of that cup? It's broken!"

I have a tendency to sit with a coffee mug in my hands when I'm in the room with a client. It's more than just steady caffeination. The warmth from the mug is grounding, and it helps control my exceeding gesticulation, to which I'm prone. This particular mug had a shattered handle, largely fractured all over, and a chip on the rim that would cut my lip if I drank from it the wrong way. Nonetheless, it was sentimental to me. Unsure of how to reply, I sat blankly for a moment. I could not think of a good counseling response that was along the same lines as "How does that make you feel?" The energy in the room became tense, and I knew I needed to respond quickly. I said the first thing that came to my mind and defaulted to an impromptu self-disclosure. My voice quivered slightly as I said, "Well, the cup was a gift from someone who I cared about deeply—and I've had it for a really long time. It's pretty unique, and I've never seen one like it before. I thought about repairing it, but I have no idea how to, and I don't want to make it worse than it already is. Besides, it still holds coffee. It's still useful. It gets the job done. I don't see any reason to throw it away because of a few chips here and there."

A serene silence took place shortly after, although I was still a little shaken by the adrenaline. I noticed that the client had a few tears calmly running down the side of their cheek. The client softly said, "Thank you," and gently walked out of the room. I didn't realize that we were already out of time.

Extrapolate what you will, but this is still by far the most therapeutic experience I have fostered, and it was completely unplanned and unintentional. However, my response held roots in my training, with influential professors who have taught me how, when, and what to say when appropriate. Trust yourself in what you do, because you've made it this far. By doing this, you will thrive.

• • •

Ng is correct. You have made it this far, so it is time to start trusting yourself. By now you have seen clients and probably transcribed a couple of your sessions. You have watched yourself on camera and hated every moment of it. Maybe you have handled a couple of crisis situations and confronted clients, supervisors, and colleagues. The thriving in this phase of the counseling program, like Ng explained, is within your ability so trust yourself.

## Preparing Yourself

It's OK if you are not mentally ready to graduate. For some of you who are reading this book and about to graduate, you could be feeling one of two things: (a) "I cannot wait to be done with this degree; I do not have any more time or money to be fooling around with another semester" or (b) "I wish I had just one more semester to soak up a bit more knowledge from Dr. Know-It-All and Dr. Down-to-Earth." If you belong to either camp, there are several points of focus that we would like to highlight as you prepare yourself to complete your third year. We discuss attending to yourself as you start your third year, transitioning from the cozy cocoon of your program to the dangerous world of prelicensure internship, and preparing yourself for the emotional release of not being considered a "student." The switch from student to colleague feels swift. Even though faculty have slowly led you up to this transition, it is nevertheless disorienting. Alicia Eggleston, a recent graduate of the marriage, family, and child counseling program at the University of Mary Hardin-Baylor, shares her experience of making the switch from graduate student to professional counselor.

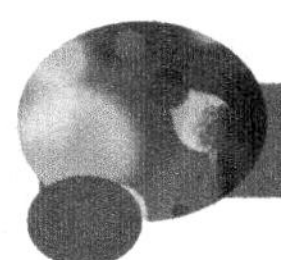

### Voices From the Field 4.2

**Making the Switch**

***Alicia Eggleston***

At what point does school switch over to career prep? I would say that point comes at a different time for each person. After all, every fire is ignited by a different spark, and your journey through the counseling program will be a fire in its own right. Maybe this ignition takes place after your first semester when your passion is affirmed by the information and stories you glean from your professors. Or maybe this happens when you see your first client—when you enter the session afraid that any wrong reflection will break the client but you exit the session realizing that you might actually know what you are doing and that clients are tougher than you (and they) think.

Beyond the consideration of when this ignition will occur, you may find yourself asking a handful of other questions such as the following:

- "How will this switch happen for me?"
- "How can I make sure this switch does happen?"
- "How will I know when it happens?"
- "What do I do once this change takes place?"

These questions should tell you that you have something very exciting to look forward to. As you start the program, you may be surprised by some of the negative thoughts that cross your mind—dreading going to class, not wanting to read your textbooks, and even wondering if this much school and money is worth it. I believe the way you will know this experience has made the switch from school to career prep is when going to class feels like an opportunity more often than a burden, professors feel more like mentors than professors, and reading your textbooks feels more like case prep than a waste of time.

I understand it may be hard to admit that these negative feelings are sometimes true, and maybe they aren't at first, because let's face it, this is a wonderful opportunity. It is one that not many people have. But even as a counseling student, you are only human. You are allowed to have these feelings. And believe it or not, some days these more negative thoughts will pop up even after the switch has taken place. In case you did not hear me before, I'll repeat it: You are only human. Life happens and sometimes you are tired, your baby is sick, or there is a flood in your apartment, and you may be struggling to view reading 60 textbook pages as an exciting opportunity.

Although life can get in the way, if you have the opportunity to get a graduate degree (and it is truly right for you), do you not owe it to yourself to see it through? There will be times when going through the program is as easy and natural as breathing, and there will be times when being intentional in seeing this program for the opportunity that it is will be your saving grace. Making the switch does not mean that going to class for 3 hours will always be fun and that reading those 60+ textbook pages will be exciting, but you will know that this is not permanent and that you are doing this for a purpose.

If you are looking forward to classes becoming more than classes, professors becoming mentors, and peers becoming counselors, you are on the right track and must be patient. When the days come, and they will come, when you feel yourself losing sight of the opportunity that lies ahead of you, you should remember that first semester when your professors affirmed your passion, that first client who looked to you for steadiness and calm, or whatever it is that lets you know you are in the right place. And remember that comparison is the thief of joy. Your fire will not burn the same as anyone else's, but that does not mean it is any less powerful. Trust the process and you will see the switch taking place right in front of your eyes; you need only look.

• • •

Eggleston's story describes when she saw herself and her experience differently. She noticed it in her approach to class—seeing the 3 hours in class as an opportunity rather than a burden. The third year is full of change, just like every other year in graduate school. This is a great time to check in with and balance yourself.

## Attending to Yourself

We know, by this point you think that you have attended to yourself more than you had hoped for a lifetime. But attending to yourself in your third year is specifically important because there is so much change. For us, the most important point of attending was making sure that we did not live in the future—thinking about life after graduation before finishing our third year. Other areas of consideration with regard to attending to yourself include

- your energy levels,
- your clinical expertise,
- your professional relationships, and
- your personal life.

Let's start with your energy levels. At this point in your career, you are thinking, "What energy levels?" If so, we definitely feel you! Think of your energy as a mobile phone that has been charged to 100% the night before. Your energy starts off the day with an alarm. Then, you open up a weather app and various social media apps, and finally you settle on a music, podcast, or audiobook app. The fight between phone calls, text messages, social media, and other apps continues throughout the day. At the end of the day, the mobile phone version of your energy has had app after app syphon energy from it. If you are like us, you tend to never remember to close apps after you use them. Thus, your energy can sometimes feel like you are being drained by all these open apps, so it is important, especially in your third year, to find ways to conserve energy.

What helped us conserve energy during this year was buying a giant dry-erase board and organizing due dates and important thoughts/questions. For some, a giant dry-erase board is a first-class ticket into anxietyville—we get it! Other organizational options are small notepads or splurging on a fancy planner. We also made hard rules regarding time. We decided not to respond to emails after a certain time or on the weekends. We actually scheduled in time to do things that would recharge our spirits, such as going for walks, playing videos games, or cooking. Finally, we got sleep. We decided to make a rule to be in bed by at least 10:30 p.m. or 11:00 p.m., and we admittedly broke that rule every night. But the intention allowed us to at least begin the winding-down process, which eventually gave us 6 to 7 hours of sleep.

Because you are still a student, it is easy to think about your clinical experience as in the distant future. But the reality is that you are both a student and someone transitioning into the professional counseling world, so you have to think about what's next for your career. Here are some questions and brief answers regarding decisions you will make about your clinical experience:

- *Is the internship site at which you are currently working going to be a viable option for collecting licensure hours?* It depends. We suggest always trying to stay with your site, especially if it's a healthy one. But if not, be intentional about the type of site and the type of clients you want to give your energy to.
- *Do you want to receive clinical supervision from someone at your site (if it's an option) or would you rather receive supervision off-site?* We suggest getting supervision off-site. There are serious consequences to dual relationships within organizations regarding supervision. Often your clinical supervisor is also your boss. So, what do you do when you need to talk to your clinical supervisor about how uncomfortable your boss made you feel about a client or case? But if your clinical site supervisor is healthy enough to manage multiple relationships with you, then carefully try it out.

- *If you plan on moving to a different state, what are the licensure requirements?* It's best to figure this out early, but we completely understand that opportunities have a funny way of showing up at the last minute. Check the state board's website, and always call the state board with any questions you might have. In our experience, our state boards have been extremely patient and helpful and have answered every single question we have had.
- *When do I submit paperwork for provisional licensure?* You submit this paperwork after comps and, depending on your state, before or after you pass your state board exam. It may be helpful to peruse the state board's website after your first semester of internship and begin the paperwork in the beginning of your second semester of internship. Work closely with your professors or adviser if you have any questions. They may be familiar with the process.
- *If you do decide to seek supervision off-site, who do you get and how much will it cost?* Get the cheapest supervisor you can find is definitely *not* our suggestion. In our experience, it is best to find one who is in close proximity to you and who also has time available for you. Try to find someone who has a similar counseling style or philosophy to you or try to find someone you want to emulate.

One crucial point is that you are in control of your own clinical experience. Often we see students who are stuck in their role as a play therapy intern because they thought they wanted to work with children but are now realizing that they want to work with the college-aged population. The temptation to stay at your established site with an established client flow to get licensure as quickly and stress free as possible is real—and we get the temptation. But it is important to ask yourself if seeing clients in a population that does not suit your career path for the entirety of the licensure process is worth it. Being intentional about the clients you see, the supervisors you choose, and the colleagues you are around is of the utmost importance, which takes us to our next point about your professional relationships.

Your professional relationships shape who you are as a person. This is a heavy statement, so let us briefly unpack it. In a professional setting, your relationships need to contain trust, compassion, humor, and boundaries. You need to ensure that these individuals will allow you to be vulnerable when making mistakes or sharing your experiences with clients. You need compassion from these individuals, especially when times are stressful or you encounter a difficult case. Humor, in our opinion, is an essential part of any relationship.

Boundaries are also important, especially with professional relationships. We look at our careers as a living, breathing entity that is in our care. Having improper boundaries with professional relationships can influence your career in an unhealthy direction. By saying that professional relationships shape who you are, we mean that they have the power to affect your career, your professional identity, and the relationship with those outside of your profession.

Regarding your personal life, attending to relationships and caring for yourself are at the top of our list. As mentioned previously, your clinical setting and those who work within it can play a major role in your attitude, your stress level, your career trajectory, income, and self-confidence. Once any one of these things are out of balance, it may cause issues in your personal life. For us, it is important that we not only maintain an appropriate balance between our personal and professional lives but also recognize when the two are out of balance and give ourselves the latitude to live within this imbalance until it is rectified. Furthermore, accepting the fact that imbalance is a natural part of life in our profession helps us to not get so down on ourselves when we are paying too much attention to working instead of playing with our children.

Self-care is important, but in your last year in the program, we would also encourage you to consider what community care looks like. As you are finishing up clinical hours at internship sites, you are probably building your community connections. In some cases, your supervisor was an alumnus from your program with his or her own connections. People in your cohort are also out in the field making connections. Everyone is plugged into the community in some form. With community care, you see yourself as part of a bigger network of clinicians in the area who are all responsible for the health of each other. There are at least nine clinicians' offices within 10 feet of my (Jude) private practice office, yet I rarely see those clinicians. We are all in and out of the office, depending on the clients' schedules. I do not know what those other clinicians are going through. Life after graduation can be isolating. We could all do a better job of taking care of each other as clinicians.

## Cozy Cocoon

There is no time in your professional counseling career when you are safer than while in graduate school. You have your institution, which provides a classroom and an environment for learning. You have several professors who make it their life's goal to help you be successful, safe, well-rounded, and emotionally stable. Your practicum and internship sites allow you to branch out into that community while also being tied to your program. If anything happens with one of your clients, you call your site supervisor. If anything happens to your site supervisor, you call your practicum/internship instructor. If anything happens to your instructor, you contact your program director and so on. Your clinical experience is meticulously monitored by your faculty to ensure that you never feel directionless regarding your steps toward graduation. This is what we call the *cozy cocoon.*

Now that you realize that you are in the cozy cocoon, here are some things that we wish we would have taken more advantage of during our stint in the cocoon:

- We would have spent more time with our professors—whether that time was spent in their offices, in the clinic, or out to lunch. It would have allowed us to know them as humans.
- We would have spent more time with a professor whose counseling style aligned with ours. We would have taken this opportunity to ask questions such as "How do you define your counseling philosophy?" "How do you know when you have compassion fatigue?" and "How do you help people and still maintain relationships with your family?"
- We would have sought out our own personal therapy with our on-campus counseling center because it was free on our campus and sometimes your professors, peers, and family just do not cut it.
- We would have watched our peers more often in our on-campus clinic.
- We would have been more transparent about our process in practicum and internship because most of our cohort probably felt just like we did.
- We would have been more intentional about trying new techniques in session while under supervision.
- We would have been open to peers outside of our cohort providing feedback on our sessions.

These seven items are a short list of a growing list of things we wish we would have taken advantaged of while in the cozy cocoon. The most important thing that we realized after being removed from graduate school is that you do not know what to ask or what you need until the moment is gone. Our advice would be to take an inventory of what you have experienced since you started your program; set a time to meet with your adviser; and have a genuine conversation about your excitements, wonderments, fears, and other questions you may have as you transition out of your program.

## Cohort Relationships

Relationships with your cohort members are tricky during the third year. You all went through so much together; now everyone is planning to spread out. The fog of surviving is lifting, and everyone is stepping out of the foxhole and wondering, "What just happened?" As you prepare to leave, you can use this time to better understand the roles your cohort members will play in your life and career. In the following sections, we briefly share our experiences and the experiences of our students and mention some healthy ways of moving past these issues in your third year.

### Discerning Who to Keep in Your Life

My (Julius) decision regarding which members of my cohort I chose to stay in close contact with after graduate school boiled down to how I define my friendships and what I need from relationships with cohorts. For me, friends are individuals who have been in my life since I was in college and have grown with me through various stages of my life. Although I absolutely loved my cohort and leaned on them at the most trying times of graduate school, our time together was very short. Yes, shared experiences can make individuals bond with each other, but I define friendships in terms of longevity. My relationships with cohort members were never long enough for me to wholeheartedly consider anyone a friend—at least not until 3 to 5 years of continued contact after graduation.

I am a long-distance friend, which means that I will probably call you once or twice a year to check in. I am intensely loyal and genuine, which means that no matter how long we go without talking, we will quickly get into the groove of our relationship. This is also what I need from cohort members whom I decide to stay close with after graduate school. I need people who do not need me to be consistent in their lives but who know that if they need anything that they can call on me. I need someone who does not play the one-upmanship game. We all know someone who plays this game in the cohort. When explaining how successful you were using a particular technique with a client, this individual says something along the lines of "I did that technique in practicum; let me tell you how I was more successful." Ultimately, I need a cohort member who will let me do my thing and I'll let them do their thing. When we meet at a conference or chat on the phone, I would hope that they know that I care for them.

The way we suggest discerning who to remain close with after graduation is by getting a feel for those individuals who want you to win without thinking that your wins diminish them. Look for individuals who genuinely want you to do well, accomplish great things, and be happy. We also suggest keeping close with individuals who were with you in the part of your training where you needed the most growth and who do not hesitate to remind you how far you have come. Finally, we suggest staying close to people who know how to make you laugh. There will be times in your third year where you will stress over internship hours, comprehensive exams, the national board exam, and many other important things. Having someone who has been through it with you and allows you the chance to reflect on moments of growth can do wonders for your attitude and outlook.

## Comparing Yourself to Your Peers

We all do it. We all compare ourselves to our peers. This comparison is not always bad. In fact, comparing yourself to your peers can spark great leaps of growth and awareness. It can also provide you with just the right amount of fuel to degrade yourself, put yourself down, or stop yourself from growth and awareness. Counseling programs have the perfect configuration for comparing yourself to others. Students usually enter into a program with a cohort system or at least with others who matriculate through the program together. Students usually take theory courses before application courses, which sets up what we have noticed to be an "ideal counselor" scheme among our students. We will take a moment to describe our experience of this "ideal counselor" that our students report to have.

Our students report something that we noticed when we were graduate students: The combination of the ethics course, the counseling theories course, and the course on psychopathology or the *Diagnostic and Statistical Manual of Mental Disorders* leads to the creation of an "ideal counselor." What we did to create the "ideal counselor" was take the most ethical counselor we could imagine, sprinkle in the most theoretically grounded counselor, and add in the most proficient diagnostician. We remember thinking that we had to be perfect in all of these categories to be the "ideal counselor." What we noticed among our students who also developed this "ideal counselor" scheme is that they began to judge not only themselves based on this ideal but also their cohort members and peers. We noticed that as soon as one cohort member strayed away from attempting to be the "ideal counselor," there was a subtle separation from that person.

A counseling program is a breeding ground for comparison, and the closer you get to graduation, the easier it is to compare yourself to others. The structure of most programs allows for the practice of clinical skills as well as the observation by others of your clinical skills. But comparison can go beyond the clinical skills learned in your program; you could compare your internship site, clinical experiences, or philosophical standings to someone else's. You may also compare a peer's position in life (e.g., getting married, buying a house, getting paid a certain amount of money after graduation) with your own. Because it is common for life to be in a holding pattern of sorts during your graduate school experience, your third year is when your peers begin to have an idea of where they will complete their licensure hours and start to plan for the future. Be aware of how easy it is to forget that everyone is on their own journey. If you slip down the rabbit hole of comparison, then it becomes harder not only to appreciate the fact that you made it to your third year and that graduation is in sight but also to be supportive of your peers as they accomplish goals they have set for themselves.

## Faculty Relationships

We know that by your third year you may never want to see your professors again! After spending so many days and hours fretting over assignments and lecture notes, this feeling is completely understandable. Maintaining relationships with faculty in your third year can be a bit tricky, especially because you are essentially on your way out. In this section, we want to provide you with healthy ways of maintaining relationships with faculty members as well as some insight into our experiences of ushering students out of the program and the way it has potentially changed our relationship with them.

First, let us start with relationship maintenance. By this point in your educational career, we are sure that you have run into several types of professors. We are assuming that you have met or at least heard of all of your professors. You will have professors in your graduate program who stay on the periphery and some who have had a profound impact on your counselor identity. Maintaining a relationship with every professor in your program during your third year is important because it broadens your network and provides an opportunity for the relationship to develop into a more collegial one.

Broadening your network is the name of the game as you move closer to graduation and start looking for a job in the profession. Your professors can be important resources for you, whether you are continuing your education, staying in your community, or moving outside of your state. Use them. Do not be shy. We cannot stress this enough. If the faculty in your program have healthy relationships with students and the community, leverage this to your benefit.

## Closing Thoughts

When thinking about the third year or your last semester, there should be mixed feelings. You may be happy to graduate but not happy to leave. Cohort relationships are important, but you need a break from everyone. If you are like us, you linger a little longer in the clinic or the hallways. The focus of this year is deciding how you want to make meaning out of this experience. For some, the meaning is made through the connections they make. For others, the meaning lies within the service they can provide to their community after graduation. Whether you are ready or not, graduation is happening, and life after graduation starts.

# Chapter 5

# Life After Graduation

If you are like us, the closer graduation gets, the more you realize how unprepared you are for the professional world. It's scary, and it's supposed to be. We guess if we had to put our finger on the object of our fear, it would relate to the pressure of it all. Small mistakes in your graduate program can be career-ending ones outside of graduate school. The phrase "I didn't know" can be an extremely expensive teaching moment as a professional. Over the past 3 years, you have been surrounded by a cocoon of support with safety nets aplenty. If you have not intentionally taken actions to strive in your graduate program, the walk across the stage can feel like a walk across a plank. Life after graduation is the real deal, with real consequences. Before you start reconsidering your life choices, understand that you are not completely thrown to the wolves. There is plenty of support for postgraduates if you know where to find it. This is the counseling field after all. We counselors are known for our GUE-I-ness; if you do not know what that acronym stands for, we hope you can swim. Get it? It's a reference to the walk-the-plank metaphor mentioned previously.

As students, we admittedly did not have a realistic understanding of what life would be like after graduation. Our graduate and doctoral programs did not completely prepare us for life after graduation, nor should they have done so. Maybe expecting them to fully prepare us was a sign of our immaturity; we discuss maturity in Chapter 7. Nevertheless, we often hear students say things such as "I can't wait to graduate and make money" or "When I'm a faculty member, I'll [insert a naive and tragically unrealistic idea]." We cannot judge anyone because we also said those same things before graduation.

For many students, life after the degree includes obtaining licensure, working as a school counselor, beginning a private practice, deciding to get a doctor of philosophy (PhD), taking some time away from the counseling profession, starting a family, and many other options. In some ways, life after graduation can feel like there are more risks and less support. It can be a frustrating, fly-by-the-seat-of-your-pants, and cringe-worthy time in your professional life. You have the skills and knowledge, yet you feel like an impostor.

In this chapter, we share our experience on life after graduation, and some of our friends and colleagues share their experiences as well. We focus on topics such as what to expect after graduation, the licensure process, career options, and things clinicians wish they had known before entering into the field. Clinicians also describe a day in the life of a school counselor, a mental health counselor, a marriage and family therapist, and a counselor educator. First, Dr. Joel Lane, an associate professor and interim chair of the Counselor Education Department at Portland State University, shares his thoughts on life after graduation and the impostor phenomenon.

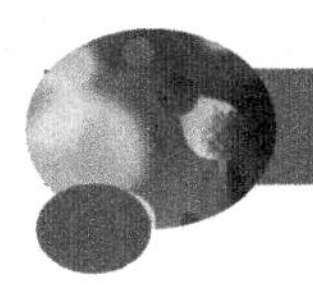

## Voices From the Field 5.1

### Feeling Like an Impostor

*Joel Lane*

Life after graduation often comes with a range of surprising emotions and experiences. The Lifespan Development Model (Rønnestad & Skovholt, 2003) is a framework for counselor identity development that has many implications for understanding the experience of recent graduates. According to this model, counselors progress through six phases of professional identity development, encompassing their time as students (i.e., the lay helper, beginning student, and advanced student phases) and professionals (i.e., the novice professional, experienced professional, and advanced professional phases). Of the many implications of the research contributing to the Lifespan Development Model, one that I've found to be especially relevant for graduate students and new professionals

> is that the transition from one phase to the next is often erratic and anxiety-provoking. This is true when I reflect on my own development as a counselor, which I found surprising because I expected anxiety to be highest in the earlier phases and gradually decrease. In practice, moving from one phase to the next (e.g., from practicum to internship, from internship to professional counselor) prompted new sets of questions and reasons for self-doubt. Sure, I succeeded in practicum, but now that I'm an intern, I'll have less oversight and more opportunities to mess up. While it may not be reassuring to learn that graduation often prompts anxiety and self-doubt, it is my experience that knowing to expect this anxiety can, to some degree, disarm its power. This experience was supported in the findings of a qualitative research I conducted on the imposter phenomenon among individuals transitioning into professional life, in which a prominent theme was that knowing about the existence of the imposter phenomenon provided important normalization and helped participants feel more competent (Lane, 2015).

• • •

In this piece, Dr. Lane explained the gift and curse of graduating. Although it is a great achievement, it can also be a source of anxiety. The graduation hood may start to feel like a yoke if you are not prepared.

## Graduation

Are your going to graduate? Are you sure? Did you check with the registrar's office to make sure you were going to graduate? Does your university have an electronic tracking system for you to check your progress toward graduation? Did you email the professor from that course that you were worried about? Be sure because as students and professors, we have shaken hands and taken pictures with students who walked across the stage but definitely did not receive a diploma. In fact, we were once those students. In preparation for our undergraduate graduation, we invited our family, told our friends, and took those awkward pictures holding those stupid hats and a fake diploma at a professional photography studio. However, a week before graduation, we found out that two online courses did not transfer, and we would have to retake an Introduction to Math course and a British Literature course. We were crushed. Don't be like us; double- and triple-check your paperwork. Honestly, we are both still half worried that even now we'll get a call from someone saying we didn't actually graduate with our PhDs.

If you are sure you are graduating, what are you going to do next? If that question makes you squeamish, welcome to the hot seat. Friends, professors, and family will ask this question a million times during graduation season. For the sake of your sanity, have a plan. Consider where you plan to live. Each state has its own licensure process. Most consist of the same procedures, but the order of those procedures can be rearranged. If you plan to live in a different state from the one you are graduating in, does that new state recognize your degree as credible? Also consider where you are going to work. Will you be able to turn your Internship II site into a job site that will help you work toward full licensure? If not, you may be looking for a new place that will give you the best chance to get licensed. Who will do your supervision? Maybe your Internship II site, which also becomes your first postgraduate position, provides supervision for free. You may also be able to find an agency that provides supervision for free. However, you may not like those supervisors and would prefer to pay for supervision that meets your standards. If you are going to pay for supervision, what are you looking for in a supervisor and how much are you willing to pay? Maybe Internship II was too much and you need some time to take care of yourself and your family. Maybe instead of going right into the race toward licensure, you decide to take some time off and receive some additional training in eye movement desensitization and reprocessing or Gestalt therapy, or maybe you apply to a doctoral program. What type of doctoral degree (counselor education and supervision, counseling psychology, doctor of psychology, or a related field) do you want to get? If you are going to pursue a doctoral degree, where are you going to live? Where are you going to work? The cycle of planning continues. These are some basic questions to get you started on planning for your professional life after graduation. The answers to the questions vary from student to student because everyone has different circumstances and career goals. Focusing on a plan for what would happen after graduation helped us find greater meaning in our training experience. We hope the following sections help you develop a plan for life after graduation. Benjamin Ng, who you were introduced to in Chapter 4, shares his experience of life after graduation, and he briefly discusses the limbo stage of the licensure process, which we will discuss further.

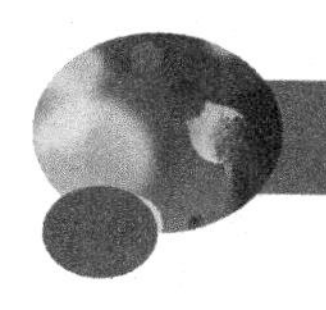

## Voices From the Field 5.2

### Go Forth and Apply

***Benjamin Ng***

You've taken out tens of thousands of dollars in student loans; read an innumerable number of journals, textbooks, and dense original texts; and sacrificed social and familial relationships by placing them on the back burner. You've pulled all-nighters writing papers and questioned whether this counseling gig was worth it, but you continued to work diligently to achieve a 4.0 grade point average (or close to it) like the good little overachiever that you are. Three years of painfully hard work have been summarized and ratified into a piece of paper that states you have a master of science, a master of arts, or a master of education in counseling, and now you're ready to use everything that your training has taught you. So, it pains me to ask you to forget all of that. Forget about everything you've learned about counseling, or at least call everything into question.

My master's degree experience had shown me what "perfect" counseling looks like—how Gestalt therapy works via the Gloria tapes, how to use cognitive behavior therapy questioning to untwine "irrational" beliefs, or how Carl Rogers was able to use reflection in such a deceivingly simple way. It all made sense! It provided me with a flowchart to direct client responses, which enabled me to deliver a "perfect" retort to foster emotional well-being. It was almost beyond belief to have canned phrases at my disposal for when a client discloses the most horrific trauma imaginable, which displaced my own anxiety about being a new counselor.

And I was hideously wrong.

My vocational life would be so much easier if my clients' progress followed the steps and models that I've so arduously ingrained. If you're working in such a myopic manner and the client responds in a completely unexpected way, your self-talk may sound like "How come I didn't get the response that I saw from the tapes?" or "Oh no, what do I say now?" Although it may be obvious, I feel that it bears repeating: What our schooling has taught us rarely translates directly into how to navigate the complexities of real clients. You may have had a taste of that during your internship, but the potent aftertaste settles in after graduation.

During your internship, your program supervisor ensures that the site upholds the standards of the university. Although there are decent workplaces that naturally uphold this standard regardless, it is most definitely not a guarantee in your first real counseling job. Gone is the typical 50-minute session for every client that you meet, as well as continued therapeutic work that spans more than six sessions (if you're even lucky enough to get that!). Your program doesn't fully prepare you for what to do when you find out your client (who was previously "treatment resistant") has run out of insurance days, and you have to break the news that you can no longer be his or her counselor (and you have to wrap up that conversation in 15 minutes because you have a group to run right after). Your program doesn't fully prepare you for when your client diagnosed with borderline personality disorder walks into oncoming traffic soon after your session. Your program doesn't fully prepare you for how to approach a group session after a group member died from an overdose the night before or what to focus on when a group member interrupts another member who was in the middle of a trauma narrative to spontaneously disclose that two group members have been steadily copulating behind closed doors. The potential scenarios are endless.

Although your program can't fully prepare you for those things, it doesn't mean that you're unable to manage them. It's true that therapy is an art. Your program has provided you with tools—paintbrushes of various sizes and a plethora of mediums such as acrylic, charcoal, pastels on canvas, wood, or paper to work with. But whatever piece you create is your own. Your program provides you with what counseling looks like under ideal circumstances, but it's your job (to the best of your ability) to fit that into whatever setting you're in. Trust that after consultation, consultation, and consultation, you will have made the right decision. Counseling is inherently grey, which gives us a lot of space to play around in.

But first—a job!

I've seen too many members of my cohort fall to the wayside because they were unable to secure employment after graduation. So, if you're willing to pursue the field of counseling, you will more than likely have to enter what I dub the "eat crap" period. Provisional licensed professional counselors, licensed professional counselor interns, and licensed marriage and family therapist (LMFT) associates are taken advantaged of: The pay will most likely be terrible, the jobs available are not going to be ones that simulate private practice (unless you were incredibly lucky or you previously sold your soul to the devil), and the clientele or work obligations may not be what you initially signed up for. Ultimately, you will question whether going into severe debt for this was worth it. However, it is in this period where I have learned the most, and I am able to say that I am a confident, competent counselor because of this experience.

Much like the way theoretical orientations develop and are influenced with the advent of time, your initial interest in school counseling may change. You may develop a fascination with substance addiction, or your passion for traditional counseling may meander into a preference for 20-minute social-focused sessions in juvenile diversion programs. Although we are creatures of habit, we learn and grow via experience, and we can't know what we flourish in without having to endure the process. You will discover your specialization when you find or validate your counseling passion. In other words, don't be picky, initially, but know what your limitations and boundaries are. Counseling is a surprisingly versatile degree; specialties in vocational/rehabilitation counseling, forensic counseling, and pure outreach/community engagement all look incredibly different than what we were initially trained in but can be just as fulfilling. By no means am I suggesting you work with a population that you may be sensitive to, nor to practice with a company that is unethical to the nth degree. I do ask you, however, to question yourself if you think, "This position isn't good enough for me; it's below me." Know your worth but make compromises accordingly. I assure you that you won't be working mental health rehabilitation/mental health professional work forever, unless that's what you're into.

So, go forth and apply to jobs! It can be discouraging. I applied to over 150 jobs during my last semester in graduate school, and I received maybe 10 callbacks, but I graduated with four job offers, which is a good problem to have.

• • •

## The Licensure Process

### Preparation

Simply put, you will have to get a couple of thousand supervised hours to get licensed. Both licensed professional counselors and LMFTs need to get these hours. But before you begin chasing those hours, start by carefully researching your state's licensure process. Each state has its own specific demands, paperwork, costs, and supervision requirements. Fair warning, it can be a bit tedious going through the state's licensure website and paperwork. Our dad's motto was "Go slow and use both hands." This basically means take your time, be patient, and use all available resources. We have gone through these websites and the paperwork for licensure several times as we've matriculated through school and sought job opportunities. We usually carve out a whole day, or a couple of days, to sit with the website and comb through all of the paperwork. We then make ourselves a step-by-step guide with notes and completion dates for tasks. The more organized you are, the less likely you will face challenges going through the process. In some circumstances, mistakes can add time to this process, pushing your prospective licensure date further back. Once you feel like you are prepared to start the process, call the board. Do not call the board at the beginning of this preparation process and say, "Hey, break down the licensure process for me." Know your process well enough to teach it.

It is hard to describe the feeling when you submit your completed licensure paperwork. I (Jude) sent off my paperwork to the state board via my local UPS store and practically floated back to my house. I received an email a couple of weeks later saying that I had an inadequate number of hours to receive permission to sit for the licensure exam. My heart dropped. Before sending off the paperwork, my supervisor and I triple-checked the documents and hours. I did more math than I have even done in my life to make sure the numbers added up correctly. I went back to the step-by-step guide and through every document since I started my graduate program. I started there because my state allowed me to carry in some extra Internship II hours. Everything checked out. I called the licensure board and spoke with the administrator who counts the hours. She was more than kind and counted the hours to me out loud. She paused and started apologizing because two of my documents were stuck together. She sent me an approval letter the same afternoon. My experience ended happily, but we have colleagues with horror stories. You have to be prepared and organized throughout the entire process—from graduate school to licensure.

## Choosing a Supervisor

When you apply for licensure, you will need a supervisor. Your supervisor is responsible for your clinical work, and he or she is basically telling the board, "Hey, I put my license on the line for this person." After signing a bunch of paperwork that amounts to the phrase "Are you sure?," you have yourself a supervisor. Dr. Gulsah Kemer, an associate professor in the Department of Counseling and Human Services at Old Dominion University, shares her advice on how to get the most out of supervision.

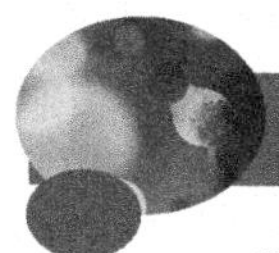

Voices From the Field 5.3

## Getting the Most Out of Supervision

***Gulsah Kemer***

In my experience, new counselor trainees very frequently fear supervision and end up not using their supervision and supervisors as well as they could. Supervision could be considered as a safe haven, while supervisors are allies of their supervisees. Supervision is the time, if there is a good one, to acknowledge mistakes and discuss those mistakes with supervisors to learn from those experiences. Supervision is also the time to recognize and embrace strengths as a counselor trainee. The more comfortable counselor trainees become with sharing their experiences and asking for feedback on the areas they struggle with, the more their supervisors can further facilitate their learning and growth. To me, supervisors are not solely responsible for making sure the supervision experience is productive and effective; supervisees must also take ownership for their learning and growth through the process of supervision. Therefore, supervisees' preparation, investment, and engagement are the most critical components of supervision, and these components are the areas where supervisees are active contributors of the process. I love to draw parallels between counseling and supervision processes to give examples. For example, think about a client who is eager to learn about themselves, is open with you in counseling sessions, initiates interaction with you, seeks out growth-related opportunities, engages and responds well in counseling, is receptive of your feedback, is open to multiple perspectives, and is willing to apply what is discussed in counseling. Sounds like an ideal client, right? Now, change the word *client* to *supervisee* and the word *counseling* to *supervision.* This person could also be identified as an ideal supervisee. Such supervisees invest in their own development as counselor trainees by preparing for supervision to their best ability and identifying the areas of their practice to discuss with their supervisors, and they engage in the supervision process with an open mind and in an interactive manner. As a result, those supervisees usually contribute to a desirable supervisory relationship in which they could increase their counseling abilities while enhancing their self-assessment and awareness more efficiently.

In my supervision practices with both counselor and supervisor trainees, I have observed specific characteristics of beginning counselors: Counselor trainees seem to feel uncomfortable (a) when they have to show their audio and video recordings, and they have a tendency to hide the moments they thought they did bad;(b) when their supervisors use counseling skills with them in supervision; or (c) when their personal functioning is explored as part of their professional growth as a counselor trainee. I believe these experiences and feelings are developmentally expected, especially because of the gatekeeping responsibility of supervisors. On the other hand, I also encourage counselor trainees to think about the reasons why they may be experiencing some of these. I believe an introspective approach to the supervision experience and practices is the first step of becoming a good counselor. What do I mean by an introspective approach to supervision experience? It is not uncommon that counselor trainees feel uncomfortable about things in supervision that their clients also feel uncomfortable about in counseling. While a counselor trainee refrains from showing their growth moments from a counseling session, a client also refrains from sharing experiences for which they feel a counselor may judge them. Thus, discussing your fear evidenced by your hesitancy with sharing your growth moments in supervision is a wonderful practice on how to broach clients' fear to share their deeper world with you or anybody else in their lives. In a similar fashion, what makes you uncomfortable when your supervisor uses counseling skills or explores how your personal issues are influencing your counseling work is also a practice of immediacy or process commentary. Supervision is not only a place to check what you did wrong or well but also a place of rehearsal, where you are challenged and pushed to grow and where most learning happens. Presence in supervision or being in the moment of supervision is one of the most challenging and rewarding tasks of supervision, one that counselor trainees are often not prepared for but learn easily. Overall, I believe supervision could be more productive and supervisors could be more effective if supervisees invest in coconstructing exploration and understanding.

• • •

Dr. Kemer's piece highlighted students' responsibility to make supervision meaningful. The supervision process after graduation could take years; time you can use to grow into the clinician you want to be. Dr. Lane shares his thoughts on the supervision and licensure process after graduation.

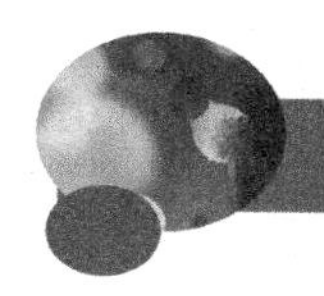

## Voices From the Field 5.4

### Supervision and Licensure

***Joel Lane***

Each state in the United States has requirements for licensure as a counselor. These requirements usually involve meeting certain educational requirements (generally the equivalent to a Council for Accreditation of Counseling and Related Educational Programs–accredited master's degree program), successfully completing the National Counselor Examination (NCE) or the National Clinical Mental Health Counseling Examination (NCMHCE), and completing a certain number of hours with clients (generally between 1,500 and 3,000 hours) while receiving clinical supervision. Typically, these requirements take a minimum of 2–3 years after graduation to complete. Depending on the state, there are different designations for counselors who are postdegree but prelicensed. Some states will issue a limited or provisional license (e.g., limited licensed professional counselor or LLPC), whereas other states will refer to such individuals as registered interns or counseling associates. It can be very useful while you are a student to make yourself aware of the licensure requirements in the state you intend to practice. I have found that a Google search with the name of the state followed by "counselor licensure requirements" will generally retrieve the information you need.

A key task during the post-master's, prelicensure period is finding a clinical supervisor. The importance of selecting the right supervisor cannot be overstated, as a wealth of research has demonstrated that the quality of the supervisory relationship is one of the primary predictors of counselor self-efficacy (e.g., Morrison & Lent, 2018). Your place of employment will play a major role in the selection of your clinical supervisor, as some job sites will provide a supervisor for you. Such situations have benefits and drawbacks. The primary benefit is that you will not have to pay for private supervision, whereas the main drawback is that you will have less choice in selecting your supervisor. If your employer does not provide you with a supervisor, then you will need to find a private supervisor on your own. Generally, supervision rates range from $70 to $100 per hour of supervision, and it is common to meet for supervision one to four times per month. The exact amount of supervision you need will largely depend on the state's licensure requirements. Some states, for example, will require a certain amount of supervision per month based on the number of hours you spend with clients, whereas other states will be less stringent and only require a total number of supervision hours by the time you are ready for licensure.

Searching for a supervisor can feel daunting as a graduate student or recent graduate. I recommend seeking supervision referrals from professors and colleagues who graduated before you and checking in with your state's professional counseling association, which sometimes maintains a supervisor registry. I also recommend interviewing multiple supervisor candidates so you can assess fit. The following are some good questions to ask potential supervisors: What is your supervisory style? What theoretical orientation do you use? How would you help me further develop my theoretical orientation? How would you be involved if I were to encounter a crisis situation with a client? It is also a good idea to ask about scheduling, fee structure, and any relevant policies the supervisor may have for their supervisees.

• • •

Supervision for licensure is different than supervision for practicum or internship. The relationship has some of the same properties, but the stakes are a bit higher. You can start looking for a supervisor as early as you want. Preparing for life after graduation before graduation lessens the adjustment period. Another part of the licensure process to prepare for before graduation is the licensure exams. Some states require you to take the licensure exams after you receive your graduate degree and others require that you take them after you have completed all of your licensure hours.

## Licensure Exams

In this section, we will cover our experience taking the three most common licensure exams you may take upon graduation or after completing your clinical hours for licensure. This small section will not completely prepare you to take the exams, but it may help you develop realistic expectations for the exam experience. Reading this section alone, without studying, will significantly increase your chances of failing these exams.

### *LMFT Exam*

I (Jude) recently did a presentation for my university's physical therapy doctoral program cohort on conversion disorder and other somatoform issues. Even in that presentation, a student asked how many tries it took me to pass the LMFT exam. This exam is infamous for failure. Some students switch their whole clinical tracks from marriage and family counseling to clinical mental health counseling because of this exam. When we started graduate school, the rumor was that the LMFT exam was almost impossible to pass. There are horror stories about people taking it five times or giving up and switching careers. A colleague of ours said, "If you come away from the exam questioning every answer you chose, you probably passed. But if you come away from the exam confident, you probably failed." We do not believe this statement is scientifically proven, but that was the case for me (Jude).

I (Jude) recently passed the LMFT exam in Texas, and it was harder than I thought it would be, but not for the reasons I initially expected. I expected it to be filled with obscure information from the small hidden print in some ancient marriage and family theory textbook that I had to get through an interlibrary loan. It was not! The exam was hard because it felt like I processed 200 cases during some marathon treatment team meeting from hell. It seemed like 90% or 95% of the test involved some type of mock client experiencing a situation that required my clinical attention. These scenarios were all familiar. They were cases my cohort and I processed in some form during Internship II. They were also ones that I may have watched while hanging out in my program's community clinic. However, the number of scenarios, in that short of a time frame, challenges your endurance more than intelligence. Once the test ended, I experienced that feeling we all probably have after a long day of swimming, where you finally get out of the water and you randomly experience sensations like you are still in the pool. For 2 weeks after the exam, I had random flashbacks to questions I was stuck on.

I would have prepared better if I had known what to expect. Without knowing, I went out and found those ancient theory textbooks, looked for the small hidden print, and tried to cram information into my brain. For about 2 months, I studied for this test like a biology exam by cramming flash-card facts into my brain. Then I paid to take a practice exam through the Association of Marital and Family Therapy Regulatory Boards website. The practice exam made me realize how ineffective my study habits were; the information was correct and valuable, but the method did not help. The practice exam, as with the real exam, does not exactly test your knowledge of marriage and family concepts. It tests your ability to apply that knowledge to practical clinical scenarios. So, I started working on making my knowledge flexible.

Instead of knowing who developed cybernetics of cybernetics and how to draw a genogram backwards while hanging upside down, I tried to understand how to conceptualize a family via the genogram alone and how to recognize feedback loops within the interactions of different systems. Diane Gehart and Amy Tuttle's book *Theory-Based Treatment Planning for Marriage and Family Therapists* (2003) provides case studies at the end of each chapter that served as my playground. I practiced creating genograms, drawing positive and negative feedback loops, theoretical conceptualizing cases, treatment planning, diagnosing, assessing for treatment and crisis, and evaluating ethical concerns.

If I had it to do over again, I would start by studying the information in the same rigid manner but with less anxiety about the small details. The rigidity of my early study methods helped me learn the information so I could apply it. However, I would have spent less time drilling flash cards into my brain and more time processing through case examples. After discussing the NCMHCE and NCE, we provide suggestions for test day that helped us and our students.

### *NCMHCE*

I (Jude) also recently passed the NCMHCE. I took the LFMT exam and the NCMHCE 2 weeks apart from each other. In case you were wondering, this is not advisable. For the sake of your sanity, mental well-being, and personal relationships, try spreading these exams apart if you can.

The NCMHCE consists of 10 clinical simulations designed to sample a broad area of competencies. Each simulation is divided into about 5–10 sections assessing your ability to gather information and make clinical decisions. Similar to the LMFT exam, this exam mimics clinical situations that you will be familiar with after you start seeing clients. However, whereas the scenarios in the LMFT exam made me feel like I was in a treatment team meeting, the NCMHCE made me feel like I was actually in 10 back-to-back sessions.

After reading a brief scenario, you will be presented with a question such as "Which of the following elements would be important in confirming or revising the presenting *DSM-5* diagnosis?" You will then be given a list of options to choose from, some are correct, more correct, incorrect, and more incorrect. For example, if you choose an answer that is the most correct, you will receive three points. If you choose an answer that is least correct, you will lose three points. All of the questions require you to choose as many answers as you think are correct.

If you have ever taken a test where all choices seemed correct and you are left feeling both confident and bamboozled, this test will be similar to that experience. To make matters worse, you cannot aim for a certain score because the exact passing score may vary from one form of the examination to another depending on the scored simulations included. It was tempting to try to count the scores, but the exam does not indicate if you received one point or three points or if you lost two or three points.

However, choosing the correct answer may provide you with more information about the case. For example, after providing the scenario, you may be asked, "What topics would you discuss during your initial meeting with the client to form a differential diagnosis?" If you choose "substance use history," the exam may provide additional information you can add to the brief scenario. This dynamic makes the scenarios live and fluid, changing as you interact with them, just like in real-life therapy.

Preparing for this exam differed from the LMFT exam prep in that the NCMHCE required both specificity and fluidity. I learned my lesson from the LMFT exam and took a practice test first from the NCMHCE test-prep website (www.counselingexam.com). Taking those practice exams provided insight into the areas where I struggled—assessment and diagnosis. My struggles were not related to a lack of skill; I struggled to grasp the volume of assessments and the intricacies of each diagnosis, especially diagnoses I rarely experienced in practice. The NCMHCE test-prep website also provides helpful tools, study materials, and questions to help you prepare for any weak areas.

After sharpening my diagnosis and assessment knowledge, I took practice exams in increasingly test-like situations until the time of the exam. Basically, I went from casually taking practice exams while watching TV to setting aside a couple of hours a day to sit, isolated, with a time clock and the practice exam. Initially, I was shocked by the amount of practice exams I failed. It made me question my competence. In my opinion, practice makes perfect. The more familiar I was with the questions and the types of answers they were looking for, the better I performed. My fatal flaw during these practice exams was reading too much into the scenarios. After reading the small basic scenarios, I would try to view the case from multiple perspectives. I would read too much into culture, socioeconomic status, sexual orientation, wind resistance, zodiac sign, and more unrelated things. When I settled down and stopped trying so hard to figure everything out, the case revealed the diagnosis, possible assessments, treatment modalities, and ethical concerns to me. Much like in session, if you sit and listen to clients, they will tell you what's hurting. If you continue to sit and listen, they will tell you how to help.

If I were going to take this exam again, I would start with a couple of practice exams to get a feel for what I need to study. Once I better understood my weak areas, I would spend some time diving into traditional study methods for those areas such as flash cards and study guides. I would then go back to the practice exams and familiarize myself with the test process. I think that preparing in this way would have helped me to think about the exam as just another test instead of the life-changing event that it actually was for me and my family.

***NCE***

I (Julius) recently passed the NCE. I experienced it as a generally straightforward exam. You show up, sit down, and get pelted with 200 questions from eight counseling content areas. The NCE consists of only multiple-choice questions; there are no diagrams or different score values for different questions and answers. The exam does not grow with or respond to your intelligence. The examination questions are derived from the following content areas:

- human growth and development
- social and cultural diversity
- counseling and helping relationships
- group counseling and group work
- career counseling
- assessment and testing
- research and program evaluation
- professional counseling orientation and ethical practice

The exam also includes questions on the following counseling work behaviors:

- fundamental counseling issues
- counseling process
- diagnostic and assessment services
- professional practice
- professional development, supervision, and consultation

The exam takes 3 hours and 45 minutes to complete and is usually administered digitally. Although the exam has 200 questions, 160 of those are scored and 40 are not scored because they are being field-tested. You will never know which questions are scored items or nonscored items. Therefore, when encountering a particularly difficult question, do not dwell on it as it may be a question that is being field-tested on the exam to gather item statistics and evaluate the performance of the question for use on future exams.

In case you were wondering, the methodology used to determine the passing score for the NCE is a modified Angoff method. This method relies on subject-matter experts to examine the test questions and then predict how many counselors would answer the item correctly. The average of the experts' predictions for a test question becomes its predicted difficulty. The subject matter experts, who also make up the NCE committee, evaluate each question to determine how many correct answers are necessary to demonstrate the knowledge and skills required to pass the exam. In our experience, if students aim to correctly answer 90 out of the 160 questions, they have a good chance of passing. So, with preparation, it is a very passable exam.

### Test-Day Suggestions

Everyone has a different experience taking the certification and licensure exams. It is essential that you pay attention to your needs while practicing and studying. Having this awareness can help you feel more comfortable in an unfamiliar environment on test day. In this section, we discuss our test-day experience and provide suggestions that may help you be more successful.

For the thousandth time, take a breath. The worst thing you can do when you sit down to take a test is get overwhelmed by the situation. Yes, passing these exams either means that you can become fully licensed or you can start counting hours toward licensure. Yes, the outcome of this exam has financial implications for you and your family. Yes, you have worked hard to get to this stage of your career and not passing the exam could make it feel like it was all for nothing. But allowing these thoughts to overwhelm you when you take the exam will cause you to fail.

Some books and study guides suggest that you get 8 hours of sleep and eat a well-balanced meal before the test. We are not saying that advice is invaluable, but 8 hours of sleep would have us feeling groggy. Eight hours of sleep may work for you. We think it is more important to ask yourself, "What contributes to me feeling most alert, healthy, and emotionally stable? Experiment with your needs while you prepare to take these exams. If pounding Oreos and milk before taking the practice tests helps you pass, then do it. Why fix something that isn't broken during the exam time?

We left early to give ourselves plenty of time to find the testing site. Once we arrived at the site, we familiarized ourselves with the surroundings. This may sound weird, but the more a place felt like home, the less anxious we were when the test started. Simply knowing where the bathrooms and snack machines were made a difference.

When we sat down to take the exam, we took about 30 seconds to a minute to discretely look at our environment. We just wanted to know who else was in the room, where the doors and clocks were, and any signs on the walls with instructions in case we needed the bathroom. Taking the test is an exercise in patience and positive self-talk. Knowing the structure of the exams and how they are scored helped to ease our minds. For example, the NCE has some field-test questions, so regardless of whether or not we were correct, we convinced ourselves that the confusing ones were field-test questions. This gave us a weird sense of calm. Finding a place of calm during these tests helped us pass. During practice tests, you may feel like you are in the zone. Try to figure out how to get yourself to this place during the exam. Once you pass the exams and collect your hours, it feels like you are finally starting your career.

## Common Career Options

Providing an in-depth discussion about the intricacies of each career option is beyond the scope of this section and book. However, we will briefly share salient information regarding your potential experience should you choose one of these career paths.

### Becoming a School Counselor

When we talk with school counselor colleagues, the conversation often turns to how unprepared aspiring school counselors are for the complexity of the position today. From these conversations, we have decided, anecdotally, that often unrealistic expectations can contribute to job dissatisfaction and burnout. Sometimes, aspiring school counselors believe that they will be doing individual mental health counseling with children in a school setting. According to the American School Counseling Association (Bray, 2019), the recommended ratio of students to school counselor is 250-to-1. However, the 2016–2017 national average was 455-to-1. Saying that it would be a challenge to see all 455 students for individual therapy during the course of a 40-week school year is an understatement.

Today's school counselors need to be prepared to fill a variety of roles in their schools. A school counselor is not just a therapist in a school; they are the hall monitors, bus duty substitutes, academic advisers, test administrators, substitute teachers, lunchroom supervisors, dance chaperones, crisis responders, parent–teacher conference organizers, liaisons between school and community, family counselors, student and family advocates, and a host of other roles. School counselors provide direct and indirect services to students, parents, school staff, and the surrounding communities. Students receive some individual counseling, but most students receive services when attending psychoeducational or process groups. Some of the common topics students face today are bullying in schools, suicidal threats, home issues, and substance abuse.

School counselors are certified and licensed educators who are qualified to address the developmental needs of all students. They use a comprehensive school counselor program developed by the American School Counseling Association to address the academic, career, personal, and social development of their students.

### Working at a University Counseling Center

A university counseling center (UCC) is more like what some aspiring school counselors think they are getting themselves into before they walk into their first middle school: working one-on-one with students. As a clinician in a UCC, you are doing clinical work with the college population. This population is students whose ages can range from 18 to 100 years old. They struggle with various issues such as depression; anxiety; transitional issues; substance abuse; relational issues; and sexual, physical, and emotional trauma.

The primary form of therapy involves individual counseling. However, some UCCs are able to sustain the clients to do group therapy. Also, like school counselors, UCC clinicians serve the greater campus community by presenting on different mental health issues for campus organizations and classes. There is usually an outreach coordinator who schedules these events. Julius served as the outreach coordinator when he worked in a UCC.

In our experience, the strength of a UCC is its interprofessional environment. This may be the first time that counselors work on the same treatment team as a psychologist, clinical social worker, art therapist, or marriage and family therapist. This can also be its limitation. With so many styles and approaches, which voice wins in treatment team meetings? We have found that counselors with a solid sense of self, personally and professionally, thrive in this environment. If you see yourself being an integral part of a college campus and working with various mental health professionals, then a UCC might be the place for you. Also, it is always nice to have built-in breaks for holidays and summer, as well as a dependable salary, which you may not get in private practice.

### Working at a Community Agency

We cut our counseling teeth at a community counseling center as graduate students. Not every graduate school has their own community training clinic, but our program did, and we benefited from seeing clients of various backgrounds struggling with many different mental health issues.

Community agency work is tough and can lead you right down the path to burnout city. The work is challenging because of the small, technical responsibilities clinicians have to manage on top of what a therapeutic relationship asks of you. The environment is much like a UCC except instead of serving a campus community, you serve all the individuals within the city or town community.

When this work is positive and provides a good experience, your caseload feels manageable, you are working with great supervisors who care about your development, your clients push you to grow in new ways every day, your colleagues are highly trained and care about clients as much as you do, and the quotas you are asked to meet do not hinder the therapeutic process. However, when this work is difficult and soul sucking, the opposite is true: The focus of the job is less on serving the community and more on meeting quotas. Your supervisor becomes a micromanager, and you are working after hours to stay afloat. Unfortunately, we hear that colleagues and past students more commonly have the latter experience at community agencies.

### Starting a Private Practice

We have recently started our private practice work, and we could write another entire book on everything we are learning in this process. When we were students, starting a private practice seemed like heaven: being able to earn a living and having a space to call your own without anyone hounding you for paperwork or any supervisors overseeing your notes and treatment plans. Private practice is different than the other options because your income is solely based on what you put into the practice. The ability to market yourself, your reputation, and the needs of your community are factors in your success.

Private practice is exactly what it sounds like. It is your private space to practice counseling. Often, licensed clinicians find a space to rent from local clinicians who have a counseling room in their building. They create their own paperwork, decorate their spaces, start a website, and get to work. Some clinicians go paperless and use websites such as Therapy Appointment (www.therapyappointment.com), which has a user-friendly practice process.

Like all career choices, starting a private practice has its positives and negatives. Some positives are setting your own hours, getting paid for your skills, growing at your own pace, and serving the community in your own way. However, one negative, especially if you are in private practice full-time, is that your income depends on many things you cannot control. For example, there are slow seasons where clients are just not scheduling sessions. Another thing to consider is whether or not to take insurance payments or private pay. Taking insurance can be complicated and overwhelming at the start. Also, private practice is a business. If you are not business oriented, you may need more support in getting things off the ground. Often your supervisor is a great source of support, as well as professors and alumni from your program.

## Things We Wish We Would Have Known and Done

After walking across the stage at graduation, we immediately wished we were not so anxious during our graduate program. We worried about grades and whether we would score high on our papers. When we walked across the stage, we weren't thinking about how we received a B in a theories course. Instead, we thought about our time in the on-campus clinic and about how hyped-up we were before our first session and then our cohort consoling us afterward. We thought about all of our friends who made huge life changes and grew in many ways throughout the program. We thought about all the time we spent in a faculty member's office just trying to figure out our lives. We thought about our first couple's session and about how we made plans with our cotherapists that never worked out in session. We thought about the number of people who genuinely cared about our growth and how we were leaving the nest. If we could do it all over again, we would sear those moments into our brains.

All students, to some degree, would describe life after graduation as bittersweet. The learning curve after graduation is steep, and most students have an understanding of what they are leaving behind. In the following section, Judith Preston, a doctoral student in the counselor education and supervision program at Old Dominion University and a therapist in private practice in Chesapeake, Virginia, describes things she wishes she had known and lessons she has learned after graduation. She shares her experience deciding to go on to get a PhD in counselor education and supervision and the lessons she learned while making this decision.

Voices From the Field 5.5

## Lessons Learned and Life After Graduation

*Judith Preston*

I am a Kenyan American who came to the United States 23 years ago in pursuit of higher education. After I completed my master's program in counseling from Old Dominion University 14 years ago, I thought about applying to a doctoral counseling program but walked away from this idea. Several years later, I revisited the idea but walked away again. I am happy to say that I am finally taking the plunge.

I decided to wait before applying for a PhD because my children were still very young. I couldn't juggle two young children, work, clinical supervision, and a PhD program. Other barriers included concerns about finances and increasing my school loans as well as the fear of applying and not getting in. I decided to focus on securing employment. My first job included work with marginalized and underserved communities. The work was overwhelming at times but rewarding and meaningful. Being a parent and pursuing a profession can stretch you thin. Create structure in your home, seek support, and find employment that supports your life.

After 3 years of working in the community and receiving free clinical supervision, I returned to Old Dominion University to take additional classes before I sat for the licensure exam. I enjoyed being back on a college campus, and for the second time, I entertained the idea of pursuing a PhD in counseling. A professor encouraged me to apply, so I weighed my options, consulted my spouse, and explored costs and school loans. I felt anxious about taking the GRE test again (I struggle in math). I wondered whether

I could effectively balance my family life and school. For the second time, I decided to walk away from the PhD. Instead, I focused on pursuing my license. I planned to work for a few more years and then revisit the idea of a PhD at a later date. It's OK to walk away from something that doesn't fit. Sometimes it's just not the right time, and letting go is a profoundly courageous act.

I passed the NCMHCE and officially became a licensed professional counselor. I was proud of my accomplishments, but I was also stressed. I was tired and often neglected myself during this rigorous process. I should have been seeing a therapist for support, but I didn't. After 5 years, the stress peaked, and I longed for change. I decided to change jobs. I needed balance and increase in pay. Work in spaces that will teach you how to learn, grow, and develop your identity as a counselor. Find a clinical supervisor(s) that will nurture and support you throughout this journey. Determine whether the work is emotionally fulfilling. Pursue jobs that are willing to pay you what you're worth. See a therapist if you need one.

I was hired and worked for a city mental health agency for 6 years. The change energized me for at least 3 of those years. I worked hard, and I developed and strengthened my clinical supervision and crisis intervention skills. I enjoyed teaching, nurturing, and mentoring other counselors. I sharpened my clinical skills. Then the stress started creeping back in. I still hadn't learned how to effectively manage my stress. By the sixth year, I was experiencing burnout. Stress and burnout will slowly creep into your life if you're not mindful about managing your stress. Changing jobs may help decrease the stress for a while, but if you haven't learned self-care practices, you'll continue to spin. Providing clinical supervision to others is a rewarding experience. Be open to learning new skills and working with new populations.

Despite feeling drained and stressed, I took on an opportunity to work part-time at a children's hospital. This space provided new insights of working with children and families in crisis, but after a while, my whole life felt chaotic and unmanageable. Juggling a full-time job, a part-time job, and parenting teenagers was too much. I realized that I was addicted to working. I needed to slow down, reflect, and reinvent a life that was manageable. Develop self-care practices that work for you. Practice, practice, and practice self-care. Acknowledge dysfunctional patterns that affect your functioning. Seek support.

I decided to create balance in my life. I left the full-time job at the agency and the part-job at the hospital. I found a job in a counseling center at a local historically Black college and university. I began to learn how to really take care of myself. I routinely practiced mindfulness, meditation, gratitude, and acceptance. I journaled, walked in nature, ate healthy, slept, and said "no." I set boundaries and created spaces of silence and stillness. I connected with myself. I returned to therapy. I tapped into niches that excited me. I narrowed my niche to treating female adult clients who were survivors of childhood trauma. I provided clinical supervision and mentored other clinicians. I started my own private practice. You can recover from self-neglect, stress, and burnout. You can reinvent your life and create balance and meaning. You can join a group practice or start your own private practice. You can give yourself the gift of therapy.

Three years in, I was experiencing my life in ways that felt present, authentic, and balanced. I revisited the idea of applying to the PhD program at Old Dominion University. This was the third and last time I would do this. I still had some reservations—my age and time—but my heart was calm and settled. I trusted myself, took the plunge, applied, and was accepted into the program as a full-time doctoral student. I started in August of 2019. I am grateful that I'll get to do what makes the most sense to me right now: academia, clinical supervision, and private practice. Trust yourself. Trust life. Hold on to your dreams and believe that at some point it might be possible to take the plunge. Define your identity as a counselor.

• • •

Preston's last sentence, "define your identity as a counselor," is something our next contributor has learned to do for herself. As we talk about ways to survive and thrive in graduate school, sometimes you make it out and your career does not go the way you planned. Natasha Villegas, an alumnus of the marriage, family, and child counseling program at the University of Mary Hardin-Baylor, shares her experience of being a stay-at-home mom after obtaining her degree.

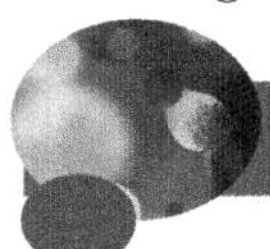

## Voices From the Field 5.6

### From Graduate School to Stay-at-Home Mom

***Natasha Villegas***

I was 23, had been married for a year, was pregnant with my first child, and was in my last year of graduate school. I could not keep my current job as a social worker, so I quit once I started practicum. This was a bold move because my husband's job did not allow us to stay afloat financially, so we saved money by living with my parents. I was a very optimistic 23-year-old and felt comfortable at the time; I wholeheartedly thought I knew who I was, and I was confident in the direction I was going. I was certain of two things. First, as a first-generation college graduate, I knew after college I would naturally apply to graduate school. Second, after graduating with my master's, I would become a professional. I was certain of these two things until I delivered my daughter 1 week before graduation and found out shortly afterward that I had failed my board exam by two points. I was in deep water. I foreclosed on the idea that life went a certain way: "If I put my train on the train tracks, then all I had to do was keep the train going in the same direction and all of the train cars would follow." But I felt like the tracks stopped and there lay no guided path. I felt confused not only because I failed the exam but also because I heard a voice deep inside calling me to stay home.

I did not realize at the time that I was changing the course of our family and making the toughest decision I have ever made. I remember outwardly sobbing to my husband as I tried to put into words my new-found journey. The wound of failing was still so raw. I put blood, sweat, and tears into these last 2 years. My mind raced; my throat tightened. I could feel the pulsating rhythm of anxiety swelling up inside me, clawing to get out. I blurted out all my racing thoughts as I continued to rock my daughter in my arms. (I know, probably not the best time to hold a baby. I hear you). Joseph, my husband, was supportive of the idea of me staying home. He said yes to what I thought was a wild idea and trusted me. Suddenly, peace overcame me and flooded the inner workings of my soul. This decision was a game changer, one that has ratified my life drastically and continues to shape the inner core of who I am daily.

After a year of being a stay-at-home mother, I failed the board exam again. Yes, we made the decision for me to stay home, but I was a walking internal mess. I constantly played mind games on why I needed to pass the board exam. I had created a narrative for myself that "to be successful you have to be a counselor." I couldn't let go of this character for fear of losing the only thing that resembled familiarity or success even if it was painful. In the end, I lost the comfort of who I thought I was and blamed motherhood for highjacking my counselor identity.

For 7 years, I have been a stay-at-home mom. I made it; we made it. The family is alive, and right now I am smitten with motherhood.

I say "right now" because honestly it comes in waves. By this point, I am obnoxiously in love with staying at home and being a momma to these tiny humans. After years of counseling, loads of insight, and another failed board exam (yes, you read that right), I just do not think life can get any sweeter. Through these last years of highs and lows, there has been so much growth in how I view myself. The strength I feel now and the motivation I have to confidently express my identity in whatever season I am in is personally freeing. I decided I was not going to let the path I originally set be my permanent destination. No, life is so much more and I can be so much greater. I simply could not let failing or fear of changing courses define the very essence of who I am and can become.

Friend, I wish at this very moment we were face-to-face sitting with coffee in hand. I would much rather be in person hearing your story, your fears, and your mountain of what-ifs as you navigate what is right for you and your family. Since we cannot, I'll leave you with this: I hope you know that no matter what path you take, you are capable, brave, and significant even when it feels like you are not. According to the film *The Curious Case of Benjamin Button,*

> It's never too late . . . to be whoever you want to be. . . . I hope you live a life you're proud of, and if you find that you're not, I hope you have the strength to start over.

Reflecting over the years and the journey of transitioning from a counseling graduate student to a stay-at-home mom has been quite interesting. I have no earthly idea what I will do with my master's degree in the future. In the very least, I hope to use what I have learned through school and life experiences to simply serve others. For now, embracing the unknown and letting life surprise me sounds just right.

• • •

## Closing Thoughts

Life after graduation comes faster than you think it will when you begin the program. In many ways, it parallels the therapeutic process in that termination starts in the very first session. When you are a student, faculty start to prepare you for graduation from the beginning. You have to do the same. Some students do not integrate the idea that their skills, knowledge, and attitude connect to their monetary value as a clinician. To say that becoming a counselor is all altruistic would be naive. We believe that you want to serve your community and also support your family. Tough decisions await the soon-to-be graduates. For this reason, at the beginning of this book, we pointed out that asking the tough, big questions early in a student's journey is helpful. Do not wait until a couple of months before graduation to figure out your professional life. The bell tolls for us all.

Chapter 6

# Getting a Doctoral Degree

In this chapter, we discuss the doctoral program experience. Graduate students have several options for obtaining a doctoral degree. The primary goal of this chapter is to provide you with an idea of what you may face if you decide to get a doctoral degree. We also discuss ways you can thrive in your doctoral program. The doctoral program, like the counseling master's program, will push you to your limits physically, psychologically, emotionally, cognitively, spiritually, and relationally. It is rewarding but presents its own unique challenges. One example of what you may face as a doctoral student is the transition from being a consumer of knowledge to a producer of knowledge. This transition can take time and involve many obstacles. Besides writing and research, you may also face the challenge of finding a mentor that you can trust. Additionally, now more than ever, competition enters the academic domain. This competition can make you feel inferior, like you are an imposter, or as if you do not belong. Doctoral students have a different set of demands, responsibilities, and cultural significance in some instances. Because of these demands, maintaining a self-care plan may take more effort now than it did when you were in the master's program.

If you are reading this right now, either you have fully committed to earning a doctoral degree or you are on the fence about it. If you are fully committed, congratulations on being in a place where you can even consider making what is sure to be a very tough decision. Just remember, you asked for this! If you are reading this right now and you are on the fence, please read carefully, and if there is anything that is intriguing or confusing, please do not hesitate to consult with other individuals who may have a different perspective than we do. Simply having the notion of "maybe I want to earn a doctorate" is massively important. It could mean creating a longer process to graduation, putting life decisions on hold, gathering more debt, and creating several different sources of income for yourself. This decision is one filled with anxiety, cultural meaning, and social significance, so you may have several questions bouncing around in your head when making the decision to earn a doctorate:

- Why a doctorate?
- How do you find a program that fits you?
- What are you willing to sacrifice in your pursuit of a doctorate?
- What if you fail?

## Why a Doctorate?

Getting a doctorate in any discipline can be a stressful, isolating, yet gratifying experience. I (Julius) did not decide to entertain the idea of earning a doctorate until the last semester in my master's program. I believed what everyone told me: "There is no reason to get a doctorate in the counseling field," "It'll cost too much money," "It takes too long to finish," or (my personal favorite) "It'll be too hard." Waiting until the last semester in my master's program to decide to pursue a doctorate was partly because of these thoughts as well as the misconceptions I had regarding the type of student that I thought goes on to a doctoral program. I thought only the smartest, most determined students go on to doctoral programs.

The reason I decided to get a doctorate is the diversity in income sources. Yes, the passion I have for educating future generations of counselors, propelling the profession forward with groundbreaking research, and shifting the image of our modern counseling textbook authorships all played a significant role in the decision to continue my education. But chiefly, I needed a route that would allow me to create several sources of income within the counseling profession. I knew that I would have student loan debt, and I eventually wanted to buy a home, have children, and travel. So, the initial idea of earning a doctorate was to maintain a faculty position at an institution while also building a private practice, writing, and consulting.

## How Do You Find a Program That Fits You?

The devil is in the details when finding the right program for you because there are so many options for earning a doctorate after completing a master's in counseling degree. Most of our colleagues pursued doctorates in counseling psychology, clinical psychology, and counselor education and supervision. We recommend you do your own research to become aware of all doctoral programs that may be the best fit for you. You can start with websites of credible organizations such as American Psychological Association (www.apa.org), American Counseling Association (www.counseling.org), and Council for Accreditation of Counseling and Related Educational Programs (www.cacrep.org) to educate yourself on what accredited programs offer students at the doctoral level. These organizations' websites also have areas where you are able to search for schools by discipline and location. You may also want to cold-call or email professionals within the field you are pursuing. Speaking to someone who has earned a degree in your field of interest may give you a window into the career in a way that words on paper or computer screen cannot. We found a program that fit us by considering three areas: environment, culture, and future.

We invite you to think about the best environment to live in. Think about the type of weather and seasons you would like to experience. As you think about the best environment, do you hear busy streets or quite neighborhoods? It is important to consider the environment that you want to live in because you will most likely be in your doctoral program for 3 or more years. We completed our doctoral degree in Wyoming because all we needed was a Walmart and an on-campus library. But we also wanted to get out of our comfort zone (anything above Shreveport, Louisiana) and experience an environment that was foreign to us. Choosing a suitable environment for you is one of the most important aspects of starting and finishing your doctoral degree, in our opinion. Because the doctoral journey is fraught with amazing successes and sometimes moments of frustration or failure, living in an environment that suits you can help make the process easier.

When trying to figure out the type of culture you want to be a part of, you can learn from your previous experience in a master's program. Think about what you liked and disliked about the culture of your faculty, program, cohort, and university. Were you professors always available to talk about grades and process experiences, or were they even physically present on campus? Was your program highly organized and supportive? Was your cohort diverse? Did your university offer adequate funding, housing, and research opportunities for graduate students? You may want to consider questions such as these when thinking about the type of culture you want when completing your doctorate.

Finally, consider your future when thinking about a program that fits you. Would you prefer to focus your energy toward clinical work? Do you find research exciting and fruitful? Would you enjoy being in front of a classroom molding the minds of our helping profession? We both chose a combination of having a sound clinical experience and developing our identities as educators. Pursuing a doctor of philosophy (PhD) in counselor education and supervision has given us the opportunity to attend to the aspects of our identities that enjoy doing clinical work as well as helping students in the classroom. Also, earning a PhD lends itself to working for a university and developing a work–life balance that fits us.

## What Are You Willing to Sacrifice in Your Pursuit of a Doctorate?

This question is difficult to answer because the answers, at least for us, were uncomfortable to admit. When you decide to pursue a doctorate, it's like everyone who matters to you embarks on the journey with you. This can be an incredible source of support for you while you experience one of the most trying educational experiences of your career. It can also bring on feelings of guilt because those who you love the most are not getting the required/accustomed time and attention from you. Are you willing to sacrifice time with your family and maybe miss important events or milestones? Are you willing to delay family plans or life goals? The answers to these questions should be examined with great care, and we suggest having conversations with those individuals whom a decision to earn a doctorate would affect.

## What If You Fail?

In examining this question, we want to take some time to express how we define failure. As you read, please think about how you also define failure. In our opinion, failure is not trying. The magnitude of people in our family who have sacrificed blood, sweat, time, energy, dreams, and tears simply to give us the option to try is at the forefront of our mind when thinking of this question. To simply not try out of a fear of failure is a slap in the face to the people who came before us. Our ancestors survived being shackled to their kin for several months during the Middle Passage, had their identities erased, and were enslaved as they watched family member after family member be sold to obscurity. They had no names, no rights, no heritage, yet they still survived unbearably harsh conditions, the Underground Railroad, the Civil War, and sharecropping. They had the unflinching strength to learn to read, write, and communicate. They experienced burning crosses, lynchings, marches in Birmingham and Selma, assignations of their leaders, segregation, omissions in textbooks and history curriculums, and stereotypes in neighborhoods and the corporate sphere. But our ancestors not only endured but also thrived in every single era to ensure that we would have the possibility to try today. Thus, for us, to not try is to fail.

## The Application Process

In the following sections, we share our process for applying to doctoral programs, but this process may look different for you depending on your situation. In general, the application process includes the following steps:

- Obtaining letters of recommendation
- Getting organized
- Seeking guidance
- Completing the application
- Interviewing
- Visiting the campus
- Being accepted
- Making the decision

### Obtaining Letters of Recommendation

For us, applying started with contacting individuals for letters of recommendation—which you want to start early in the process. We chose people who (a) had a track record of communicating back swiftly, (b) knew who we were professionally and had the type of career we wanted to carve out for ourselves, and (c) knew us on a personal level—someone who had transitioned from being our professor to our colleague and could speak to our character and personality. Your job is to provide your references with (a) the link to the program's website, (b) your curriculum vitae, (c) a brief synopsis of why you are applying to this program specifically, (d) an idea of your research interests (if applicable), and (e) your plans to use your doctorate in the profession.

## Getting Organized

Once you have secured at least three to four individuals to write a recommendation letter for you, it's time to get organized. For us, getting organized meant creating a list of schools and application materials needed with little checkboxes next to the item and writing them on a whiteboard. For example, we placed our first-choice school in the first slot on the whiteboard and next to it we listed the required materials for that program (e.g., cover letter, letters of recommendation, curriculum vitae, application fee). As we acquired the various pieces, we checked the item off the list. This helped us to be aware of things that we still needed to complete or items that were pending.

Getting organized for the application process also requires an ideal timeline of events. We suggest using the following timeline to aid your application completion process:

- *June and July:* This is a good time to understand which standardized tests are required for your program. Most doctoral programs require their applicants to take the GRE. During these months, you should become familiar with the testing requirements and begin to acquire study materials. Starting the groundwork early is beneficial, especially in case you need to retake this exam for a higher score.
- *August and September:* During these months, you begin to narrow your list of schools. Keep in mind the various factors that play a role in this decision—location, goodness of fit, structure of the program, program requirements, and so on. It would also serve you well to gather information about important deadlines, support services, program contact information, program and university fees, and application requirements. You may also want to check in with individuals who are writing letters of recommendation for you, just in case they need a reminder of deadline dates or need any pertinent information. Finally, create an application budget because you will more than likely have to pay to submit your application.
- *October:* A letter of intent or personal statement may be required for your doctoral program. Use the entire month of October to create this document. We know that taking the

whole month for this seems redundant, but this is an important document. It gives the reader an insight into who you are, so creating multiple drafts with individuals whom you trust to proofread them is important to the application process. Keep in mind that it is important to convey how your acceptance into this particular program relates to your professional goals.

- *November:* The application process begins! Be sure to visit the program's website for a list of materials needed for the application process. During this month, you should have your GRE, letters of recommendation, and personal statement completed. You may want to call or visit the registrar's office of your current university to obtain an official copy of your transcripts or arrange for the official transcripts to be sent to the doctoral program you are applying to. Organization is the name of the game during this process; be sure to fully complete each application and include all necessary documentation.
- *December:* It may be beneficial to create a master list of applications and cross each university off your list as you complete the submission process. This last step is optional, but what helped us feel secure was personally calling the doctoral programs that we applied to and receiving confirmation that they had received all the application materials.

## Seeking Guidance

It's not simply a paper application that you are completing; it's the creation of several potential futures for yourself. For example, when applying to a doctoral program, you may consider living expenses, lifestyle changes, the weather, and proximity to family. If you are like so many others deciding to move forward, you may have even taken it upon yourself to scout out apartments, homes, or other living options in the cities of the universities you have applied to. You go through these considerations for every single program you apply to because there are so many possible outcomes to moving forward with your education.

The possible outcomes are tough to sift through on your own, so that's where seeking guidance comes into play. As card-carrying members of the millennial generation, our initial reaction to "guidance" is a very precise Google search. You can find statistics about living expenses, lifestyle changes, the weather, and proximity to family in a matter of minutes. But one thing that we wish we would have done is communicate with individuals who already lived and worked at the universities on our list. A call to a clinician who works in the area can tell you much more about the clinical climate of the potential city. A call to an academic adviser can inform you about the admissions process. A call to campus housing may inform you about the availability of graduate housing or other options for students who decide to stay off campus. These calls serve two purposes: (a) You can glean useful information about the functions of the community, university, and the doctoral program; and (b) you also get an idea of the type of people you may encounter at the university. Regarding the latter purpose, you may get an impression of the university staff's friendliness, their willingness to converse with you, and their openness to questions that you may have. A doctoral program may be your first choice until you contact several departments within the university and they leave you with a sour impression of the university.

## Completing the Application

Before completing a doctoral program application, get a feel for the program's website. While perusing the website, ask yourself the following questions:

- Is information easily found?
- What information are they advertising?
- What are the required courses?
- Is there a recommended doctoral course sequence?
- Is there an application fee?
- What are the application deadlines?
- Do I apply via mail, email, or online?
- Are there preset interview days so that I can plan?
- What items do I need to complete the application (e.g., curriculum vitae, GRE scores, personal statement)?
- Is there a graduate student handbook?
- How clear is the practicum and internship process (if applicable)?
- What are the program and student outcomes?
- How many doctoral students graduate on time?
- Does the website give any indication about the dissertation process?

After these questions are adequately answered, it might be a good time to start the application process. Most universities have an online application process, but you should also pay attention to other application requirements. Some programs require that you complete an online application as well as send additional documentation to the department chair or human resources. The online application process may look similar across all the programs you apply to, and you may be required to disclose personal information such as your address, contact information, and ethnicity and race.

## Interviewing

Congratulations! If you have reached this part of the process, then that means the doctoral program thinks you may be a good fit. Here are a few steps to consider before and after officially hearing word that you have been invited for an interview:

- If you are invited to multiple program interviews, then consider prioritizing which program you would most likely attend if the interview dates conflict. You should communicate this to the doctoral program you are choosing not to interview with.
- You may have to cover travel expenses. Please inquire about the reimbursement process by phone or email before making travel arrangements.
- Collect information about the structure of the interview by contacting the doctoral program directly. You may need to ask questions pertaining to dress code, location of the interview, and interview process. Knowing information such as this can aid in your ability to feel comfortable during the interview.
- Create a list of two or three questions that you might want to ask each faculty member just in case you find yourself in an individual interview. It strikes a positive chord when you know a faculty member's research interests and how you would like to collaborate.
- Meeting with current or former students within the program is a great way of getting an insider's experience. You may want to contact the doctoral program and inquire about this possibility.
- Develop an elevator speech: Think about stepping onto an elevator with a faculty member and having 15 to 30 seconds to answer a question such as, "Why do you want a doctorate?" or "Why would you like to attend this doctoral program?"

These steps are important because you are essentially trusting the doctoral program's faculty with your educational and professional development. Yes, you are being interviewed for a possible position in their doctoral program, but a part of your experience during the interview process needs to be exploring the healthy and unhealthy aspects of the universities you visit. Gathering as much information about the program as you can while also having an opportunity to see the location, the faculty, and the campus culture aids in the decision-making process.

## Visiting the Campus

I (Julius) visited two universities during the interview process, and I learned several important tips. My first visit was to the University of Wyoming in January, and I wore my cute, little Louisiana winter coat. For those of you who have not been to Laramie, Wyoming, in January, it's cold and has an altitude above 7,000 feet. Tip 1: Contact the program beforehand and inquire about the expected weather conditions. I arrived at the university 1 day before the interview. In that 1 day, I was able to walk around the campus and get a feel for the weather and altitude, and I explored the city and scouted potential places I could afford to live. I also found potential grocery stores, gas stations, car mechanics, restaurants, coffee shops, and other places that I would need to survive during my time in the doctoral program. Arriving early gave me an opportunity to walk around the campus without being in that interview mind-set. Tip 2: Arrive early.

The morning of the interview, I showered, dressed in my finest (and only) suit, and went over the information I had stored in my head about the program, the faculty, and why I would make a great doctoral student. I arrived on campus waiting to be grilled about research interests, teaching experiences, my theoretical philosophy, and all sorts of gut-punching, anxiety-producing questions. I got none of that. The faculty brought all seven candidates into a room and asked us personal questions pertaining to who we were as people, what we wanted out of the helping profession, and what were our fears and excitements. I left the group interview thinking, "What in the hell was that and why do I feel like the interview has not started yet?"

We moved from the group interviews to individual interviews with a faculty member to whom we were preassigned. I spent the night before combing over my assigned faculty member's curriculum vitae and making note of items I wanted to broach during the individual interview. I highlighted specific questions about the program, the university, the campus; it was going to be a jammed-packed interview. Breathing heavily, I walked into the faculty member's office and sat at a table. Before I uttered a word, the faculty member asked, "So how can we get you to choose the University of Wyoming?" I could actually hear everything I prepared for this interview leave my head, and what replaced it was the thought, "Choose the University of Wyoming? I am in my only suit freezing my nose hairs off trying to get you to choose me!" So, I stumbled over my words for an eternity, which in reality was only 1 or 2 seconds, and said, "Adequate funding." Tip 3: Know exactly what will make you choose a doctoral program because you may be directly asked about it.

The University of Wyoming's doctoral interview process contained a group interview where I was able to meet all of my future cohort members; an individual faculty interview; a campus tour with current and former doctoral students; and dinner that night with faculty, staff, and potential doctoral students. I left the university feeling like I was already part of the family. I knew each professor by name, was able to talk to current students about their experiences, and spent time with everyone outside of the campus environment.

The second university I visited, which I decided not to attend, was in my home state of Louisiana. Let me put this decision into context: My whole family lived 2 hours away from this university, my significant other was attending law school a couple of miles away, and I was guaranteed a graduate assistantship if I was accepted into the program. Taking the campus visit seriously is important because it can make or break your decision to attend the university if you listen to your gut. Tip 4: Listen to your gut.

The interview process for this university consisted of one 30-minute interview with all of the faculty and a therapy session with a mock client. As I stood outside of the conference room, I remember going over the information about the program and faculty trying to ready myself for any question they could throw at me. I felt more nervous about this interview because I felt like I only had one shot to prove to the faculty that I was capable of being a great candidate for the doctoral program. I walked into the room, sat at the head of the table, took a deep breath, and thanked everyone for inviting me to interview. As we went around the room for introductions, I took comfort in the fact that I recognized some of the faces in the room. Tip 5: Visit the program's website or search the faculty on social media to get a feel for the way they look or their career interests.

The interview started with one of the faculty members saying, "We've seen your paperwork, and we like you. Why [name of the university]?" I listed off the reasons for choosing the program, mentioning the ways I would like to collaborate with faculty in and outside of the program. They asked several other questions pertaining to my research interests and career goals and then turned the interview over to me. I asked several questions about graduate assistantships, funding, and the type of doctoral student they were looking for. The answers to these questions were positive; I felt excited about the funding options and caliber of student they wanted. Then I asked about curriculum structure, graduation rates, average time to complete the degree, and common issues doctoral students face that could create issues in the dissertation process. The answers were concerning because the vibe I got in the room was "I'm not going to say anything negative about the program." I had a gut feeling that they were hiding something from me or avoiding the true nature of the doctoral program experience.

After the interview process, I was asked to demonstrate my clinical skills in a mock therapy session. The program head led me out of the building and told me, "I really hope to see you in the fall. Give us a call if you have any questions." That was it! No campus tours. No individual interviews. I did not get a chance to see how the faculty interacted outside of the work environment. I left feeling like the experience was incomplete. That night I emailed the program director and asked if I could possibly meet with a faculty member individually to answer some brief questions that came up after the interview process. During this meeting, I asked the faculty member to go into more detail about the curriculum and the process that most doctoral students take to complete their degree. The faculty member stated, "Classes are kind of like a confusing spiderweb; you might have to take some classes in different departments on campus." The university's website did not say "confusing spiderweb" under the curriculum page. I knew that I needed a curriculum structure so that I could plan for my future, and a "confusing spiderweb" screamed of unplanned delays and unexpected curriculum changes. Additionally, during the 30-minute group interview, faculty members—some of whom I would need to work closely with during the doctoral program—felt cold and distant. Tip 6: Know what you need from a program.

I have no idea what would have happened if I had chosen the second university I interviewed at, but my gut told me to be cautious based on my experience there, so I chose the first university. It was paramount that I trusted my instincts when choosing a doctoral program and that I was present during the experience—tuning in to how I felt in the environment and how the environment affected my mood.

### Being Accepted

Admissions criteria for doctoral programs can include letters of recommendation, letter of intent, phone/virtual interviews, on-campus interview, related public service, teaching experience, previous research experience, counseling experience, and standardized test scores. Also, the weight of these items may vary depending on the needs of the university or program. The hard work of deciding where to go begins once you are notified that you have been accepted by one or many doctoral programs. There are several practical factors at play during this time that you need to personalize. For us, the important factors were (a) comfort with the program, faculty, and peers; (b) the length of time to completion; and (c) funding options. We suggest giving yourself space to express your most important factors in choosing one school over another.

### Making the Final Decision

Consider that the consequences of this decision do not fall solely on your shoulders. In choosing the first school I (Julius) interviewed at, I essentially chose to live thousands of miles from family, experience weather that I have never experienced before, live in a completely different altitude, and subject those who care about me to a day's worth of flying to spend time with me. This decision will affect your family members, friends, peers, and colleagues. This decision will influence your professional career, personal life, education, and personhood. Take a deep breath and make your decision.

## Surviving and Thriving in Your Doctoral Program

Why are you getting a PhD? Find a good answer—one so good that when you want to quit it's strong enough to keep you fighting. Surviving as a doctoral student, in our experience, takes street smarts. You need the ability to read a room and know who has a beef with whom and how you could be affected by this climate. Survival is part political and part grit. Most of our friends, colleagues, and friends of friends chose to leave their programs. They decided not to finish their doctoral degree on their own terms, not because they were kicked out. We believe a doctoral degree is very obtainable if you have the determination.

Thriving in a doctoral degree program is a different challenge. In our experience, thriving in a doctoral program has nothing to do with the program itself. Often, doctoral students who thrive in their programs establish connections and garner opportunities outside of their programs. These are the students who knew about the grant application before you did. They volunteered to serve on regional and state counseling boards. Having connections outside of the program can help support healthy boundaries between you and your peers and faculty. It gives you the room to not take things personally and to feel like there is a world outside of the program, and it gives you hope that you will finish.

When students think about tackling and finishing a doctoral program, they will often use the dissertation as the deciding factor. Some say they could not write that many pages, whereas others are afraid of the defense. Dr. Gil Lerma, a therapist in the CAPS for Counseling Services office at Tulane University, shares her experience of writing and defending a dissertation. She discusses some of the ways in which she overthought the doctoral process and the ways she misunderstood the experience early on.

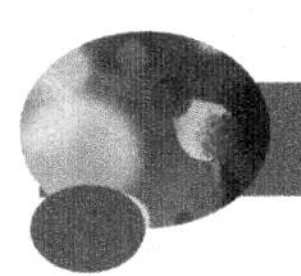

## Voices From the Field 6.1

### Advice for Writing and Defending a Dissertation

***Gil Lerma***

So many times when it comes to writing a dissertation, I feel it is quite common to hold the dissertation up as being this huge prestigious "monument" that needs to be absolutely perfect. I feel this creates a lot of unnecessary stress and anxiety within doctoral students that eventually hinder progress. In many ways completing a dissertation is prestigious, but it does not need to be perfect. I remember during the first year of my doctoral program our director spoke to my class and gave us a piece of advice that I found to be particularly helpful. She told us that when it came to choosing a topic and conducting research, "Do not make this your life's work because you'll never finish. We want you to finish, graduate, and then you can do your life's work." She went on to explain that if we treated our dissertation as our life's work, we would never finish because we would always see flaws in the research and in our writing, and we would then continuously try to perfect everything. Therefore, we would never finish and graduate.

I kid you not, as soon as I heard my director utter those words, my first thought was I'm only shooting for one to two steps over the line that determines whether I pass or fail. I will produce a good product, but I don't care about making my dissertation a perfect masterpiece. Regardless of how good my dissertation is, at the end of the day if my committee gives me the green light to defend, then I'm going to defend. I want to finish, graduate, and move on. Hearing my director explain the aforementioned information to our class really reduced the tremendous amount of stress and anxiety I felt, and it allowed me to feel a bit more positive with choosing my topic, conducting the research, and writing. So, do not try to make your dissertation your life's work!

Thinking about defending your dissertation can be super stressful and anxiety inducing. I mean that's the last step that decides whether you pass or fail. Another helpful experience I had in one of my classes was the time one of our professors explained to us that there is no reason why we should be scared of defending our dissertation. Naturally, when he said this, we all looked at each other in great bewilderment. I mean the defense is ultimately what decides if we pass or fail. How can that not be absolutely terrifying? He later went on and explained that we should not be scared during the defense because we are literally the most knowledgeable person in the room on the topic. He said, "You did all the research and you conducted the experiment. We (the professors/dissertation committee) didn't do the research or conduct the experiment. Therefore, you are literally the most knowledgeable person in the room on the topic."

Additionally, he explained that our dissertation committee members don't know every aspect of everything we are doing. They are there as resources to guide our work, but ultimately they do not know as much as we do about the topic and the experiment. Once again, hearing this information took another load of stress and anxiety off my chest. Does this mean that I wasn't anxious as hell when I walked into the room with my committee and others who wanted to see me defend my dissertation? No! I was very nervous, but I used the advice from my professor to lower my anxiety. At the forefront of my mind, I kept focusing on the fact that I am the most knowledgeable person in the room on my topic. I did *all* the research. I conducted my experiment, and I know the results of my experiment. All I have to do is explain what the research says, explain everything about my experiment, and explain my results. That's it!

One of the biggest things you need to learn as a doctoral student is setting realistic expectations and creating balance in your life with regard to your academic, professional, and social lives. If you're studying anything related to mental health, then you are already familiar with the importance of creating these things. My doctoral program was designed to be completed in 3 years by full-time students who already possessed a master's degree in clinical mental health counseling, marriage and family therapy, or school counseling. I already possessed a master's degree in clinical mental health counseling; therefore, I decided I would finish the doctoral program in 3 years. Working at the doctoral level is definitely more demanding than at the master's level, and I prepared myself accordingly. I planned to keep working full-time because I needed the income, and I planned to keep my very busy social life as much as I could. I completed the first 2 years of my program quite successfully without having to make many changes to my work schedule or my social life. However, during my third year, my life definitely changed, and it needed to change. Conducting my research and writing was turning out to be much more overwhelming than I had anticipated, especially since I was still taking courses, working full-time, and maintaining an active social life. At the end of the fall semester during my third year, I decided to complete the program in 4 years. I found myself feeling completely overwhelmed in all aspects of my life, and I couldn't take it anymore. I was barely sleeping at night, and my alcohol use was going up as a way of dealing with all of my stress, especially with the stress of graduating in 3 years.

Once I finally decided to complete my program in 4 years, not 3, I felt so much more relaxed because I was going to have so much more time (mainly because I would be finished with all of my courses) to devote to finishing my research, conducting my experiment, and completing the last few chapters of my dissertation. Additionally, I decided I really had to make changes to my social life so that I could have even more time to focus on completing my dissertation. I remember that I told all of my friends and family, "Please don't ask me to do anything. Please don't be upset if I don't return a phone call or text message." I went on to explain to them that working full-time and being a full-time doctoral student is very stressful and demanding and I needed to focus more on my dissertation so that I could finish. They were very understanding and respectful of my wishes. As a result of making this appropriate change to my social life, I was able to graduate at the end of my fourth year. I'm very glad I was able to be honest with myself about what I needed to help me finish my dissertation and that I decided to make that change to my social life. Therefore, be honest with yourself about what you need that will assist you with your dissertation journey and make the necessary changes.

• • •

As Dr. Lerma explained, sometimes people place too much reverence or respect on the doctoral process. Although it is difficult to obtain, a doctoral degree can be filled with support. Going into the program humble and open to the experience helps. Our next contributor, Laura Capasso, a doctoral candidate in the counselor education and supervision program at the University of Northern Colorado, shares her experience of going into the doctoral program with high expectations of herself. As she explains, sometimes surviving and thriving happen during different seasons of the doctoral experience.

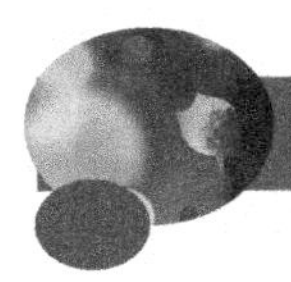

## Voices From the Field 6.2

### Ivory-Tower Perspectives

***Laura Capasso***

I showed up late to the first day of my doctoral program. I walked into the conference room and noted an official-looking woman, whom I recognized from interview day, in the chair at the head of the table. In high-backed chairs on either side of the table sat those I would soon come to know as my colleagues (a.k.a. future trauma-bonded individuals). I took my place in an open chair between two people, knowing (because I know counselors) that if I had done what I wanted to do and occupied the chair at the farthest end of the table, I would instantly be asked to move closer to the group. I made it my mission to take up as little space, literally and figuratively, as possible. This was to be a success. This was to survive.

It was when my professor began to speak that I first recognized the seriousness of the space I had entered into. Pens began moving at a furious pace around me as people took notes on the syllabi they brought (because of course they did), while I sat there empty-handed (because of course I did). I can only presume that they were taking notes about deadlines for liability insurance, hours logs, client start dates for practicum, and library student ID cards—all procedurally valuable information that I, undoubtedly, would not remember. I do remember, however, being less struck by the content of the discussion (which, as I predicted, I don't remember) and more struck by the process and the context. Why were each of these individuals so very aware of what they should be doing? Why did they all look so fancy and professional? (Buying an iron moved to the top of my to-do list, yet 5 years later, I still don't own one.) Why did they nod their heads in understanding and chuckle at jokes whose punch lines I couldn't even pick out of the fabric of conversation? Hadn't we each gone through master's programs of similar length, content, and intensity? Hadn't we each sat across from clients, acknowledged our own traumas, and used these experiences as propellers to navigate our ways into this room? Where had they stumbled upon this magical treasure of knowing, and would I ever find it too?

This wasn't the first time I had asked myself these questions. As a matter of fact, the collateral information of life had often been lost on me. As I sat there in my moderately wrinkled, artificial silk shirt, which I thought was quite fancy, I quickly became hypervigilant around my own perception of my positionality. I, the penniless, late, young girl had found myself on the lowest rung of the hierarchy of this room. I had an inkling that this is where I belonged and where I would remain. At this moment, a kind man leaned over, concerned, and offered me a pen from his own stash. I gratefully accepted the pen before asking for paper too. My face burned with the rising shame of inadequacy for the first, and unfortunately not last, time in my doctoral career. It was here that I decided not only to shrink my existence to a specific set of dimensions but also to never need another pen from another colleague again.

There is a portion of me that is acutely aware of the potential reaction to these words: duh, for example. A person showing up to the first day of their doctoral-level training should probably come on time with a writing utensil. I share this anecdotal narrative not for the sake of shirking responsibility or begrudging the appropriate expectations around professionalism. Rather, I share to illustrate the shift in spirit that I believe many experience in higher education. Shame-induced panic pushed me, swiftly and painfully, into the harsh reality of the expectation of never needing another's pen. In the field of counselor education and supervision, doctoral training is the constant verbal message to show up. Be; don't do. Engage with a de-emphasis on technique and an emphasis on mindful presence as a means of intervention. But also don't forget to write a proposal for this conference, study for a year for this written exam that decides your progression, and know that production is valued over presence. Trying to reconcile the messages of operating within productive shame so as to operate safely and successfully as a doctoral student while also operating within relational vulnerability became my (impossible) mission, my (impossible) goal, and my (impossible) identity. It felt like that was the expectation of me, and I was going to do it as effectively as any doctoral student ever had. Now, this was certainly an exercise in futility. It wasn't until the biggest tragedy of my existence, however, that the futility became glaringly obvious.

Directly in the middle of my second year of study, my baby brother passed away. I immediately communicated, angrily, with my faculty that I would not be returning to school. I was quitting. I became furious about the amount of time and life I had traded for living in the ivory tower, built with bricks of shame, self-doubt, isolation, emotional distance, confusion, mixed messages, incongruence, hierarchy, and feelings of never being enough. I began dismantling and hurling these bricks at passerby, faculty, family, and friends alike. I was struck, in the worst way, by the functionality of these bricks in the world of academia. I saw, as I examined each brick, one by one, how they had worked to insulate me from the life around me. As painful and perhaps damaging as this may have been, it woke me from the zombie-like faux existence I had been living. I had lost my brother, and that was everything. No longer could the real or perceived disapproval of a faculty or cohort member cause my cheeks to burn with shame that determined my identity. No longer was the pursuit of the initials PhD a good enough excuse to turn away from the pain and lived experiences of my loved ones or myself.

My doctoral program has been one of the most painful, enlightening, and worthwhile experiences of my life, in part because I believe it has prepared me well to do the work that I love, in part because I have explored depths of myself I didn't know possible, and in a larger part because walking through it has taught me how to turn earnestly and shamelessly to the person beside me and ask for a pen.

• • •

Capasso showed that doctoral students do not have it all together either. This should show you that no matter where you are in your counselor development journey, you do not have to have it all figured out either. The challenge of the process is to be OK with that and love yourself through the growth. This is a crucial element of taking care of ourselves, as our next contributor, Sarah Silva, a doctoral candidate in the counselor education and supervision program at Walden University and a therapist in a group practice in Chicago, Illinois, points out.

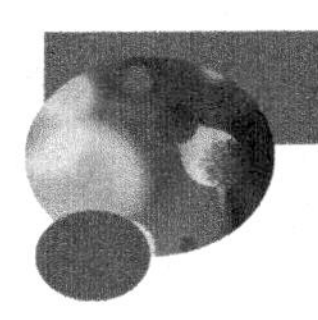

## Voices From the Field 6.3

### Maintaining Self-Care While Earning Your Doctorate

***Sarah Silva***

The truth is that maintaining self-care as a counselor is tough. But I'd bet you already knew that and have experienced how difficult it is to maintain a self-care practice as a clinician. You've got all of these responsibilities, client demands, emails, documentation, clinical supervision, and a boss you may or may not be too fond of. Imagine all of that with the added pressure of earning a doctorate! It can be extremely hard to fathom, and I recall a time earlier in my doctoral program when I asked faculty how they maintain balance and take care of themselves while practicing as a clinician, teaching full-time, mentoring, researching, writing book chapters, and so on. I imagine that as you read this right now you may be wondering, "What did I get myself into?"

Maintaining self-care while earning a doctorate is like putting a 3,000-piece puzzle together all at once. It sounds incredibly impossible, and I imagine you're already feeling the pressure from your peers, professors, employers (if you work through doctorate), and loved ones (who are proud and probably have no idea what getting a doctorate is like), not to mention the added pressure to read a ton, write in perfect APA format, present at conferences, work on your curriculum vitae, write a dissertation, and apply for full-time faculty positions.

You'll most likely be rationalizing all of the ways to avoid self-care during the next few years because "I can hold it together; I'm a counselor." However, doctoral students need self-care more than anyone. To be quite honest, we may actually need more of it when we go through a doctoral program because of all of the added pressures. Sure, the coursework may seem manageable at times and incredibly interesting, but it can also take a toll on your well-being. One thing I was sure about upon entering a PhD program was that I had to take care of myself if it was going to work. I'm going to let that soak in for a bit. I *had* to take care of myself for it to work.

And that's what I did. I would plan out my week and make sure to schedule in times and specific activities I could do to destress and rejuvenate my own energy. It was hard, and there were times I let self-care fall by the wayside. But those times I didn't focus on incorporating self-care were also the times that I felt unproductive and lazy, craved fattier foods, and honestly felt really stuck and unsure of what I wanted for my future. I was on autopilot, and I began to lose the motivation and hope for being a counselor educator.

Think about it like this. If you are able to find the time and energy to dedicate your life to completing a doctoral program, you also *need* to create time for yourself. As a counselor, you know this. But knowing and following through are two different things.

As awesome as you are at maintaining self-care right now, self-care will usually be the first to go when you're focused on getting through your doctoral program. Each step of the doctoral program will present new challenges, changes in levels of time commitment, and more reasons to let your self-care practices go. And usually it's for a good reason; you want to be a counselor educator. So, even when you have peer-reviewed journal articles to read (we all know those can be draining), edits to do for your dissertation, papers to write, or conference proposals to write, any form of self-care you thought you were good at *will* go out the window.

So, I'm asking you to do something that seems simple in theory and extremely difficult to do in real life. But it works! I would like you to schedule self-care into your calendar/planner each week and each day, even if it is just for 30 seconds. Find activities that fill your own bucket that take 2 minutes, 30 minutes, 1 hour, and so on, so that you have a variety of self-care activities to choose from when you are crunched on time. I want you to stop reading right now and take the next 30 minutes to plan out some self-care activities for your week. And I want you to stick to it. You'll find that when you stick to a schedule of incorporating self-care despite being busy, you're much more productive in your doctoral studies, and you'll enjoy and embrace your doctoral studies more and more. Trust me, I did not think it would work either. I can say that my doctoral journey has been incredibly transformational and rewarding because I spent some time on myself. So, hold yourself accountable because no one else is going to make you do it, even if you have an accountability partner. And this is coming from someone who ran a group practice with three locations while teaching online and in person and attending a doctoral program full-time. It's time for you to take your own suggestions that you provide to clients.

• • •

## Closing Thoughts

This chapter focused on the doctoral experience. It, like the master's experience, can be a challenging and rewarding part of your counselor development. You have to decide why you are putting yourself through this experience. Dig down deep and find something to cling to when it gets tough. The difficulty ebbs and flows in this experience. One season you are thriving and the next is pure survival. Giving yourself the space to be in those seasons helps you stay healthy. There is no point in getting a doctoral degree if it's going to ruin your health and destroy your family. Be mature about this decision. Do not do it just to be called doctor—although it is nice to hear.

# Emotional Maturity

By now, you probably have a better idea of what you are getting into emotionally as a graduate student. You should understand that although you will learn some great skills and improve your knowledge, you get your money's worth in your personal growth. The more you push yourself to grow, let down your guard, and exist more genuinely within relationships, the higher your emotional maturity rises. Think of your personal growth like a muscle: The more effort you put into growing it, the more you can rely on it when you are processing difficult cases.

Start by reflecting on where you are emotionally right now. Try to be as honest as you can with yourself. Avoid asking, "Am I ready to start a counseling program?" No one is ever *ready* to start a counseling program. Before you read our definition of emotional maturity, define it for yourself. Develop a picture of yourself as an emotionally mature person; how close are you to that ideal self?

This chapter focuses on emotional maturity—this intangible characteristic within all students who become the clinicians that faculty members trust to work with their own families. Faculty members look to accept students with high emotional maturity above emotionally immature students. In this chapter, we break down the concept of emotional maturity and provide some tangible suggestions on how to grow into this characteristic.

## What Is Emotional Maturity?

Emotional maturity is a complex facet of the person we try to develop in our counseling programs. It has elements such as emotional stability, emotional intelligence, self-awareness, awareness of others, and receptivity to feedback. A student's emotional maturity is observed through their thoughts and behaviors. When faced with the complex challenges of becoming a counselor, a student's level of emotional maturity is a major determinant in his or her ability to cope with the stressors of the counseling profession. In some cases, a student's inability to mature emotionally throughout the program can result in removal from the program. This may seem harsh, but it is a curtesy for the student and the community.

One of our biggest fears as counselor educators is having a student slip through the cracks. Maybe we are not paying close enough attention to that student's development, or the lack thereof. Maybe that student is doing a great job of pretending to grow and hiding his or her weaknesses. Letting students who are not emotionally mature graduate can cause great harm. They could be put in a clinical situation that could be triggering or retraumatizing, or they may not have the maturity to accurately assess a crisis situation.

So, what is emotional maturity? Emotional maturity is the student's ability to respond to his or her environment in an appropriate manner. From the perspective of a counselor, an appropriate response is one with genuineness, unconditional positive regard, empathy, and immediacy. It also involves responding to what is actually happening in the environment, not what is filtered through past hurts or a need to manipulate others. An appropriate response is generally learned rather than instinctive and is not determined by a student's age. We have all known that 10-year-old child who has an old soul and just seems solid already. We have also known the 50-year-old adult who has a fragile ego and always seems to be overly affected by things.

We want students to graduate with such a sense of solidity in their character that they are not overwhelmed when their environment throws them a curve ball. Do not misinterpret this to mean that you have to be a Zen guru who is always living in the present moment, nonjudgmentally and unflappably accepting everything that happens. Solidity means that you intimately know what affects you and how to respond in a way that does not hurt others. Emotional maturity is characterized by a genuine interest in doing things for their own sake, to give love to others without an expectation of receiving something in return. According to Crow and Crow (1962),

> an emotionally mature or stable individual, regardless of his age, is the one who has the ability to overcome tension to disregard certain emotion stimulators that affect the young and view himself objectively, as he evaluates his assets and liabilities and strive towards an improved integration of his thought, his emotional attitude and his overt behavior. (p. 107)

To better understand Crow and Crow's explanation, we provide some characteristics of emotionally immature and mature graduate students. Here are some characteristics of emotionally immature students:

- *High emotional reactivity:* These students typically hold the belief that life just happens to them. They struggle to take responsibility for their actions or current life circumstances.
- *Emotionally acting out:* In other words, these students act out without filtering the emotions that are inside of them. Some might say that it is impossible not to do this in life. However, emotionally immature students act without reflection, especially when experiencing a perceived threat.
- *Inflexibility:* These students hold onto who and how they are, even when their environment is screaming at them to change.
- *Self-preservation:* These students only look out for themselves. Even if your program does not operate using a cohort system, you still need others to be successful in this profession. We believe that you are only as successful as those with whom you graduate and enter into the profession. They are your referral sources, consultants, and battle buddies.
- *Avoiding discomfort:* Discomfort is a common aversion. It is rare to find a student who is excited to jump right into the middle of a fishbowl activity in front of the whole class and do a mock therapy session. However, students who are so afraid of failure and rejection that they never push themselves outside of their comfort zone struggle to mature.
- *Isolation:* In the counseling program, we grow within the context of our relationships. Growing into emotional maturity becomes more challenging if a student's defense mechanism is to alienate from others. We encourage students to get involved in their program, attend mixers, meet with faculty, join the cohort Facebook group, and stay connected.
- *Living in the past or future:* Students who want to become a counselor because of unfinished business in their past can deter their development if they hold on too tightly to those issues. The saying "we get the clients we need" has never been truer than for stu-

dents who live in the past. Likewise, students who hold on to the notion that they *must* become an ideal counselor or professional equally deter their maturation. Letting go and allowing the process to work on you is the best way to approach the journey.

Here are some characteristics of emotionally mature students:

- *Proactive:* These students take responsibility for their actions and choices. If a project is due at the end of the semester, they start ahead of time. If they need support, they contact their adviser before their issue becomes a crisis.
- *Reflective actions:* These students act with awareness, not instinct. They tend to put more thought behind the decisions they make.
- *Purposeful:* Although they do not have everything figured out, these students tend to understand the importance of graduate school and intentionally take actions to make their experience meaningful.
- *Considerate:* These students think about others as much as themselves when they act or react to things in their environment. They reflect on questions such as "How am I affecting you?" "What's going on for you right now?" "How is this affecting me?" and "Am I responding in a way that pushes this person further away instead of closer?"
- *Courageous:* These students push themselves outside of their comfort zones. They volunteer in class demonstrations and are willing to be vulnerable. They process real, deep, emotional content in supervision and are receptive to feedback.
- *Growth seeking:* These students go above and beyond to grow into the clinician they want to become. These actions do not have to be big or expensive; they can be something as simple as reading an unassigned but related book, attending a professional conference, or experiencing a webinar.
- *Living in the present moment:* These students tend to relate to others and their environment on multiple levels: physically, psychologically, emotionally, spiritually, and relationally. This characteristic ebbs and flows from moment to moment throughout the course of the counselor's development.

## What Level of Maturity Is Necessary to Get Through Graduate School?

To get through graduate school, you need a level of maturity that grows as you face each challenge the program presents. You do not have to come into a counseling program self-aware and actualized. Just come in humble and ready to work. The work starts early in your training because the program asks you to manage your time and integrate a large amount of information. Then your level of maturity needs to grow when you see your first mock clients and real clients during practicum. Your level of maturity needs to grow even more as the program pushes you more and more into the profession during your final internship class. In that class, you may feel isolated or even abandoned by your faculty as your caseload grows and faculty involvement decreases. The idea is to push you gradually into independent practice. It helps if you have some characteristics of emotional maturity coming into the program.

If you are like us, you have probably watched enough movies that depict graduate students as coffee-drinking, frantic workaholics who run around campus with loose papers falling out of their leather satchels. This may be true for some students, but for the most part, graduate counseling students are moms, dads, veterans, former athletes, police officers, and other hard-working people who are just trying to serve their communities. You do not have to come into graduate school being anything more than just who you are. The process of the program and the interactions with faculty members and clients will push you to be more.

When you read the characteristics of emotionally immature and mature students in the previous section, you may have created a score sheet in your head, ticking off the characteristics you did or did not meet. Keep in mind that the preferred characteristics are ones that you grow into. Because each student has his or her own unique set of characteristics, it is essential that you sit down with your adviser and develop your own growth plan. Figure out with your adviser where you want to be when you graduate and how to get there. Some students have more work to do than others do, but everyone will grow as a person in the program.

## Emotional Stability

Emotional stability is a student's ability to manage both pleasant and unpleasant emotions. For example, you are assigned a client that gets on your last nerve. You may have a strong dislike for this client, but can you also empathize with this client? Can you share your dislike for the client in session, but in a way that fosters therapeutic intimacy? Emotional stability asks students to hold polarized emotions inside of themselves as they emerge and balance them. Stability starts with awareness. Tapping into your own emotional climate and identifying and differentiating these polarized emotions is the first step. The second step involves visualizing the two emotions like two sides of a scale and then processing (on your own or with others) how to balance the scale. This process takes practice. This practice is important because throughout the course of a therapy session, students experience a myriad of emotions that may compete against each other for dominance. If you are able to sit in the center of the emotions and while listening to both sides act with awareness to facilitate the therapeutic process, your work will be better for it.

In our experience, emotionally stable students are able to calmly and assertively say no. They do not overcommit, and they cannot be coerced into doing something they do not want to do. They are able to set appropriately firm boundaries with others. Emotionally stable students do not seek perfection but embrace their flaws. They do not try to be the perfect therapist; they simply try to use what they have to be effective. Emotionally stable students are also emotionally independent, meaning that their sense of self-esteem and self-efficacy are not tied to how others perceive them. We also believe that emotionally stable students are comfortable with silence. The do not need to fill the space with small talk as a way of managing their anxiety. Emotionally stable students also fully understand and accept that they will lose friends in their journey to become a counselor. They keep their inner circle tight and have a heightened awareness that the company they keep influences them. This stability allows students to be more attuned to themselves and their clients. It increases their emotional intelligence.

## Emotional Intelligence

Emotional intelligence is the student's ability to recognize others' emotions through subtle cues and use this awareness to handle interactions empathetically. This facet of emotional maturity is your grandma's special power. Maybe it's just our grandma, but she always seems to read people by how the wind blows an eyelash or some other outlandishly tiny detail on their face. This is a learned ability that comes with experience. It's what some call street smarts. You can walk into a room and read the vibe. You can taste the tension or levity.

Emotionally intelligent students simply think about and prioritize feelings and their impact. These students are curious about the subtle interactions between individuals. They may seem quiet, but they are just pausing to take in their surroundings. They also express their authenticity, but not at the cost of others. They have the ability to carve out their existence in relationships without diminishing another's existence. Emotionally intelligent students can also provide helpful feedback. They may actually be more aware of the kind of feedback someone needs to hear or is able to receive in that moment. Emotionally intelligent students apologize when they make mistakes. This display of humility can strengthen therapeutic relationships more than displaying confidence. Finally, how someone treats an emotionally intelligent student does not determine how that student responds. For example, students interact with many individuals in various different emotional states. If a client comes into session angry or rude, it would not help to respond in kind. Having emotional stability and intelligence allows students to respond with empathy and respect and meet clients where they are.

## Self-Awareness

Well, it took us long enough to get to a section covering probably one of the most important traits to develop in graduate school—self-awareness. (It's better late than never.) Given everything we have covered in this book so far, you may already have an idea of what self-awareness is and why it's important. Self-awareness is critical. It is more than just knowing yourself. Self-awareness is a process of developing a deep understanding of your own needs, desires, failings, habits, strengths, and everything else that makes you unique.

Imagine a piano tuner working on a piano, playing each key repeatedly until they are all tuned and working together to make a melody. Then imagine that each key is a different element of your character and you are the piano tuner in your life. The tuning process is the self-reflective process needed to develop self-awareness. You have to play each key and listen to how it sounds alone, how it sounds compared to other keys, and then how those keys sound together as they reverberate in the environment. Also, because who and how you are is always in flux and every life experience throws you slightly out of tune and changes you, you need constant retuning. We want you to be able to go through life acutely aware of when something within yourself feels right and when it does not. When you are in session and feel off your game, we want you to be able to pull yourself out of the process briefly, check in, and notice what is happening. You might be getting triangulated, manipulated, or experiencing countertransference.

Working in this profession without self-aware is dangerous for you and your clients because of how involved you are in the process. The therapeutic relationship is unlike any relationship in your life. The line between personal/sexual intimacy and professional intimacy is razor thin sometimes. Navigating these dynamics takes focus, awareness, and intentionality.

To better grasp the importance of awareness, imagine this scenario: A clinician is in an unhappy marriage. She was not taking care of herself and her caseload was higher than usual. She starts working with a male client in her age group whom she finds attractive and with whom she gets along well. That client is also unhappy in his relationship and feels a connection to the therapist that he has not ever experienced with other women. One day during session the client asks the counselor how she is doing. Maybe he makes an observation about her seeming unhappy. The therapist bites and overshares her personal life experience. The client, after watching the therapist reflect his content and feelings for 6 weeks, attempts to comfort the therapist. The therapist feels a spark. She is in private practice. No one would have to know if they got to know each other on another level.

You may be cringing as you read and thought through that scenario, but it is all too common. Unfortunately, little research is done on the frequency of this boundary crossing because clinicians don't openly admit to ethics violations. You can find yourself in the same situation as the therapist in that scenario if you lack the awareness of how your personal life influences your professional life, your personal and relational needs, and the relational dynamics within the therapeutic relationship. All of the money and time spent getting your counseling degree and license will be for nothing because of actions without awareness. Erotic transference is only one example of why it is so important to develop self-awareness throughout your training. Other reasons include (a) when clinicians take more responsibility for the work in therapy than the client, (b) when clinicians push their agenda in session (for example, maybe there is a form of therapy they really like such as mindfulness or sand tray and the client is just not into it but they insist the client try this kind of therapy), (c) when clinicians impose their values onto clients, and (d) when clinicians engage in advice giving or finger wagging. Although these actions are common and normal responses, they should be avoided. The challenge in growing into emotional maturity through self-awareness is to decrease instinctual reactions and increase intentionality.

Another challenge facing students when developing emotional maturity is thinking they are not good enough to become a counselor. Woodside, Oberman, Cole, and Carruth (2007) found that counseling students view their training experience as saturated with self-doubt. Martha Thomas, a graduate student in the clinical mental health counseling program at the University of Mary Hardin-Baylor, shares her experience of self-doubt and how she turned her age, which she thought would be a weakness, into a resource.

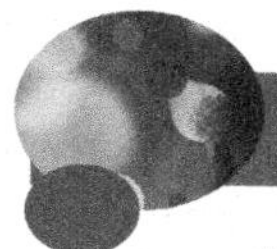

Voices From the Field 7.1

## Going Back to Graduate School at 50

***Martha Thomas***

Getting my graduate degree at age 50 was one of the best decisions I have ever made. I was a stay-at-home mom for 22 years and was fully present for all that that entailed. I loved it. I knew my goal, my mission, and my duties, and I had an amazing partner in my husband, Brian.

After my oldest child went off to college, I grieved for a year. After some good healing time, I applied for graduate school and started classes 6 months later. I wanted and needed a new direction for this next chapter in my life. The choice to be a mom was a dream come true, but after that job ended (or more truthfully, lessened), I was unsure where to go or what to do.

I had been thinking of starting the graduate counseling program at University of Mary Hardin-Baylor for a few years. I felt like that is where God was leading me, but the timing was always off.

I honestly think that going back to school at age 50 puts me at a greater advantage than younger students because of my experience in living life. The older I get, the more I realize I have so much to learn. I have enough wisdom to know that I am only an expert on my own experiences and outside of that I do not know much at all. Raising two kids and keeping them on track and helping my husband with his professional/personal to-do list has taught me to handle several things at one time. It has given me confidence to do things. I am not sure my younger peers in the program have as much experience in these areas as I do. It is only because I have been alive longer than they have. I have always tried to be a lifelong learner.

There have been both challenges and successes. I am not as technically savvy as my younger classmates. I don't understand the pop culture references of the students who are 22–35 years old. My son is 22, and sometimes I feel like I talk to my classmates like they are my children. (When I am frustrated, the mama in me comes out.) My younger classmates haven't failed and learned in the ways I have. It is often extraordinarily frustrating to be in class with someone who is asking several questions of the professor and all the answers are found on the syllabus. I am not as academically "in shape" as my younger classmates. The learning curve was steep for me to get into the habit of taking good notes, reading and comprehending the textbook, knowing what to study, knowing how to write a paper, and knowing how to navigate school. That being said, I find that I am a great student. This has been a complete surprise. As an 18-year-old, I just sailed through college without studying hardly at all and received a very deserved 2.6 GPA, but I got a degree (in education) and a job and that's all I was trying to do. Now, I am passionate about learning. I love exercising my brain. For all of my life, I thought that I was just "too emotional" and basically stupid. But now I know differently. I love school, learning, and making good grades. I want to do these things for myself, not in competition with others. I want to do the very best I can. I want to be successful. Finding intrinsic value in achievement is a strength that only comes with experience and age. It is a strength that I am blessed enough to have repeated and encouraged by my husband. Brian often tells me he believes in me and completely supports what I am doing. He tells me that I am smart and that he is proud of me.

My family is both an advantage and a disadvantage. I love my family, and I would lay down my life for them. I am passionate about having a relationally, spiritually, and emotionally healthy family but that is also my greatest weakness. Even though both of my sons and my husband have repeatedly told me that "it is OK with them" for me to be in school, I still feel guiltily and selfish for focusing on my continued education, especially when the needs of my children bump up against my needs as a student. They tell me that I am a good role model for them and watching me study so much encourages them to study hard as well. They tell me that they like learning to do things on their own and being challenged to become more independent. They tell me that they like hanging out with their dad and having "all boy" time. But still the guilt lingers.

Another advantage of being older is having the ability to communicate and connect well with different kinds of people. Also, I am not intimidated by my classmates or professors, although I am intimidated by the amount of knowledge I need to learn. I am not spending my free time looking for a boyfriend or navigating a relationship that is uncertain. I am not dating or looking for my "forever man." I am not going out drinking and partying. I am often exhausted at the end of the day. I go to bed early every chance I get, and 10–12 hours of sleep seem to be the right amount for me right now. I also realize that my classmates have a lot to teach me. I never really understood Google Docs, but now I realize that it is an amazing tool. As an undergraduate, I used a typewriter to write my papers, and I had to use an actual card catalog in the library and walk down the stacks of books to find what I needed. To take research materials home, I had to Xerox pages out of books. I had to write out class notes and mail things via the post office. College life, information, and most other aspects of being a student move so much faster now.

My advice to others who want to start graduate school at 50 is go for it! Going back to school has been absolutely one of the best things I have done for myself. I am a better person, mother, and wife. My family has benefitted from my growth, and I have benefitted from this experience. I would *not* have been able to come out of graduate school with as many positive qualities if I had gone straight to graduate school after my undergraduate degree. I am almost a totally different person at 50 than I was at 25. I did not have the emotional capacity to be a serious student the first time in college. At the age of 22, I was so broken emotionally from my childhood that I was just surviving life. The healing I've experienced through counseling, being married, having children, and living life has brought me to the place where I am now ready to learn, discover, grow, and be all that I can be. This school experience has strengthened me. It has broken me down physically, mentally, and emotionally, but it has shown me that I have a greater strength within myself, more than I ever knew. I am confident in myself. My ability to make good grades has redefined a part of myself. I trust my voice, which I found while in graduate school. I already had a mom voice and a wife voice, but the Martha voice was not fully formed. I now have a voice for myself, and I enjoy using it.

• • •

In summary, emotional maturity is a complex characteristic that counselors grow into. Part of this growth is developing emotional stability and intelligence. When we peel back the onion a bit more, we see that self-awareness and self-reflection are at the core of emotional maturity. If emotional maturity was a car, self-awareness would be the engine and self-reflection would be the wheels. Although we look for emotional maturity in students when they interview to be accepted into the counseling program, students do not have to have it all figured out when they arrive. This characteristic needs to be forged. Increasing it within yourself takes work that may be done over the course of your whole career. Some ways to increase your emotional maturity are to (a) wake up and be present to the things around you, (b) embrace reality (work on all of that unfinished business you have with your past so it does not ruin your future), (c) take responsibility for your stuff (your agendas, perspectives, values, and opinions), and (d) maintain integrity (know yourself and be yourself while leaving space for others to be themselves).

## Closing Thoughts

The focus of this chapter is one that dominates faculty discussions when we are deciding who to admit to our programs. Does this student have the emotional maturity to survive the rigor of this program? This chapter covered some specific characteristics of emotional maturity. Growth is vital, and it is assessed constantly throughout your time in the program. Some of this growth happens as a byproduct of attending class and supervision sessions. The big relational changes occur when you push yourself to grow within the relationship of your family of origin and close relationships outside of the program. Emotional maturity gives you the ability to overcome setback, which is a natural part of this profession.

Chapter 8

# Dealing With Setbacks

Setbacks are inevitable in the journey to becoming a counselor. It may take some students five tries to get accepted into the graduate program of their choice. Other students may be asked to repeat a class, be given a behavior contract, have to withdraw from classes, not get the internship site they wanted, or not get chosen for a clinical position they and their family needed. Setbacks can cause a considerable amount of stress and pain as well as influence our self-esteem and work with clients. In this chapter, we discuss setbacks that we and our contributors have experienced throughout our journeys. We hope that this discussion will prepare you for what to expect and build your resilience when you experience setbacks along the way.

## What Is a Setback?

A setback is a check or reversal in progress. A setback is inevitable while on your educational journey. It accompanies anger, frustration, and possibly shattered hopes. It also may be the exact occurrence you need to propel your journey forward. When graduate students encounter a setback, they often go through the following process: mourning, guidance, perspective, and action.

### Mourning

Mourning is a time to give yourself permission to feel—whether those feelings are anger, fear, terror, or being overwhelmed. Take time to experience the setback and breathe, cry, laugh, or deal with it in a way that's most natural to you.

### Guidance

Guidance is the part of the process where you go back to the people who provide support and encouragement to you. Following a setback, you can experience a real pain, one that can be debilitating to your spirit. Connecting with someone who supports and guides you can provide perspective.

### Perspective

Perspective often occurs after you have had some distance from the initial shock of the setback. During this part of the process, you can begin to understand and learn from the setback.

### Action

Action is the time when you may take what you have learned from the setback and begin again or start something new. Any type of change in the graduate school process is tough, especially if it influences your timeline. This time may provide you with an opportunity to slow down your process and make the best of your setback.

## Types of Setbacks

Throughout the graduate school, students encounter several types of setbacks. Some of the more common setbacks include, but are not limited to, being overworked, self-sabotage, loss of motivation, and unhealthy feedback. In the following sections, we discuss these common setbacks and the influence they may have on your educational journey.

### Being Overworked

An essential part of being a graduate student is the familiar feeling of bring overworked. Because you are trying to balance your professional life and personal life, you may feel pulled in many directions.

During our time in the internship portion of our graduate program, we juggled the clients on our caseload, our course assignments, supervision, research projects, and a personal life. It got to a point where even talking to our family members became chores. Feeling overworked has a way of creeping up on you when you are no longer intentionally present.

### Self-Sabotage

Self-sabotage comes in many forms such as agreeing to too many obligations, setting unrealistic expectations, and comparing yourself to others, and these types of self-sabotage are insidious throughout graduate school. Graduate programs have built-in obligations such as course assignments, but there are instances where agreeing to research opportunities, learning opportunities, or opportunities to connect with your peers may prevent you from taking care of yourself and your educational responsibilities. Setting unrealistic expectations can also be a part of the graduate school experience. Telling yourself things such as "I guess I'll have to pull an all-nighter," "I can write this 20-page paper over the weekend," or "I do my best work under pressure" are unrealistic expectations. In addition, comparing yourself to others is also a form a self-sabotage. It is quite easy to compare ourselves to the students who make it look easy or the professor who always knows the right thing to say in a mock session. This can create negative self-talk, doubt that prevents creativity, and barriers to learning.

### Loss of Motivation

Motivation ebbs and flows throughout the graduate school process. At some points you may be highly motivated and full of enthusiasm and optimism. There are also times when you may feel deflated, like the wind has been taken out of your sails. Setbacks can act as conduits for conveying half-heartedness and detachment from your experiences. Setbacks raise the question, "Are your goals worth dealing with whatever setback you encounter?"

### Unhealthy Feedback

An important quality of being a graduate student at any level is receptivity to feedback. Feedback about your coursework, relationship to peers, and clinical work can be given throughout your time as a graduate student. As a student, you can either take this feedback personally or simply let it go into one ear and out of the other. But unhealthy feedback is something that's deeply personal and unique to each person. In our experience, unhealthy feedback is laced with the giver's own insecurities or biases without taking your personhood into account.

## Handling Setbacks

Imagine acquiring an internship at a coveted internship site. You turn down offers from other sites you applied to and begin the preparation process of entering this new experience. A couple of weeks before internship starts, the site informs you that due to budget cuts they will no longer be able to provide you with an internship position. From your perspective, this internship site would have allowed you to eat, pay your bills, and graduate on time. Setbacks such as these can have very real consequences on your educational path and life circumstances. There are several ways to deal with setbacks before they arise or after they are upon you: (a) Take care of yourself, (b) be creative, (c) ask for help, and (d) know when to take a break.

Taking care of yourself is one of the simplest and also hardest things to accomplish throughout graduate school. At times, we put in longer hours than necessary, eat unhealthy foods, and lose connection with those who are dear to us. Taking care of yourself by incorporating breathing exercises into your life, changing your sleeping habits, and experiencing nature can all help the recovery process after a setback.

Being creative is another beneficial way of dealing with setbacks. Doing creative projects such as drawing, painting, and creating music are all suitable ways of dealing with setbacks. However, thinking of unconventional solutions to setbacks and using your imagination to possibly foresee setbacks you may encounter along your journey may also help you deal with setbacks. Creativity can help you develop alternate approaches to setbacks that may help you navigate your needs versus your environment's needs.

Asking for help can be humbling at times, especially if it is not something that you tend to do often. Help in situations where you are experiencing a setback is paramount to the process of dealing with the setback. Help from others can provide you with moral support, consultation, supervision, and a shoulder to cry on in the toughest of times. When setbacks arise, individuals who have similar experiences may offer support and suggestions regarding your experiences.

What if you feel like you have exhausted all options regarding dealing with a setback? You have tried all of the options previously listed, and you have done your own research and tried to follow those suggestions, but nothing seems to help. Should you take a break? Should you stop altogether? Before you make any hasty decisions that may affect the trajectory of your educational career, take a deep breath. Recognize that dealing with setbacks takes time and patience. Taking a break or stopping altogether because of a significant setback may actually be a better option for you, but your situation needs to be examined carefully. Consulting with friends, family, loved ones, advisers, and professors is something that should be done before taking a break.

## Setback Aftermath

When I (Julius) was earning my doctorate, I had several meetings with my dissertation committee. I had two major meetings: the prospectus (where we went over the first three chapters of my dissertation and decided what worked and what I needed to alter to move forward and complete the research) and the dissertation defense. During the prospectus meeting, I had a committee member who mentioned that the only way she would "OK" my going forward with the dissertation process was if I changed my research methodology, and my committee agreed. This was a major setback! I felt like I had been following the directions of my committee regarding my chosen methodology throughout the writing process. I checked in with everyone at various points to ensure that we were all on the same page. I remember feeling frustrated, isolated, overwhelmed, and quite frankly angry at everyone involved. The person who I was most angry at was myself because I naively went into that meeting thinking, "I may have a few edits, but I do not think it'll be anything serious." There are several considerations for the aftermath of a setback: You should expect setbacks and not try to avoid them. After a setback occurs, take responsibility for it and replay the setback.

Looking back on the prospectus meeting experience, I could have expected different levels of edits, which would have prepared me for the possibility of needing to revise my methodology. Also, I could have met with my committee members more often throughout the writing process to ensure they didn't have major suggestions. I wish I had taken more time in developing the prospectus document specifically looking for potential setbacks. Knowing that setbacks are inevitable, I could have had outside individuals provide feedback to lessen the changes I would need to make. Simply entertaining the idea that my methodology could be changed as a result of this meeting was too scary of a thought, so I avoided it. Avoidance, in this situation, played a major role. I allowed the success I experienced early on in my doctoral program to create this idea that I was immune to major setbacks.

For days after my prospectus meeting, I blamed every one of my committee members. I blamed my dissertation chair for not protecting me in the meeting and not silencing the committee member who suggested the change. I blamed my methodologist for not catching this possible change in the editing process of my methods section. I blamed the committee member who suggested the change and thought that it was a personal attack. I refused to take responsibility for my document and the shortcomings it had in successfully arguing for my proposed methodology. The sooner I took responsibility for my role in this setback, the easier it was for me to take a deep breath and salvage some good components from my prospectus and begin the editing process.

I replayed this meeting over and over again, asking questions such as "Why did this happen?" and "What could I do to ensure that a setback like this does not happen again?" Additionally, I examined myself and concluded that being humbler and open to not having all of the answers could prepare me for future setbacks. I used the experience in my prospectus meeting to inform my decisions throughout the rest of the dissertation process. Setbacks such as this can help you plan for the inevitable future ones and turn them into an opportunity to learn.

## Closing Thoughts

In the words of Dr. Ray Eary who you were introduced to in Chapter 3, "it's best if you make disappointment your best friend instead of running away from it." The screw-up fairy comes for us all, waving her wand of misfortune liberally. This will always happen when trying to get a graduate degree in counseling. While you juggle everything, grow, change, become healthier, and improve your skills, life moves on. Setbacks will happen. This chapter covered things to look out for regarding setbacks and ways to manage those setbacks. Remember, the faculty are watching. OK, we did not mean for that to appear as creepy as it did. The faculty members are watching and willing to walk alongside you in those setbacks, not punish you for them. Lean on the faculty as much as your friends and family. Try not to wait until the issue is critical before reaching out to them.

# Managing Conflicts

A common misconception about counselors is that we are the masters of our emotions, relational experts in our personal lives, and all emotionally mature. This belief could not be further from the truth. The demands of graduate programs can strip students down to the essence of who they are. There is an inherent element of vulnerability as the undercurrent of this journey. In some cases, this vulnerability brings out the worst in ourselves and others.

Students will undoubtedly have to be in close proximity with individuals (teachers, other students, administrators, supervisors, or clients) they do not like. It is important to remember that conflict is natural and happens in every ongoing relationship. Conflict signifies that there is a need for change and an opportunity for growth, new understanding, and improved communication. Because conflict is unavoidable, students must learn to manage it. This chapter focuses on common sources of conflict that master's students may face throughout their journey and ways to manage these conflicts.

## Confronting Yourself

You are probably the one person you will have the most conflict with throughout the counseling program. Like we mentioned in earlier chapters, each facet of the training program shines a light on different sides of who you are. Confronting yourself means that you see your flaws and are accountable for them. The only way for a therapeutic relationship to thrive is for you and your client to take an honest look at yourselves and work on changing the things that make the counseling process difficult for each other.

Let's take self-doubt and anxiety, for example. We have experienced these emotions in graduate school, especially when seeing our first clients as we discussed in Chapter 3. After my (Jude) first week of seeing clients, I needed to have what our grandma calls "a come to Jesus" conversation with myself. I needed to confront the self-doubting and anxiety-filled boy inside of me who was getting in the way of my clients' work.

I remember talking myself through the sacrifices my clients made to attend session each day. I focused on the courage it took for some of my clients to sit in front of a complete stranger and share their stories, some for the first time. Realizing that turned my anxiety into motivation. I wanted to be the counselor my clients deserved. I became less preoccupied with myself and my performance in session and developed a more balanced preoccupation that included myself, the clients, and our relationship. The trick to self-confrontation is doing it without condemning yourself.

No one likes to confront themselves. The outside world does that every time our social media feeds update. Self-confrontation is scary: What if you don't like what you see? What if you have to take responsibility for things, or even worse, what if you have to make changes? As long as you are willing to compassionately look within yourself, self-confrontation can be a healthy practice. Here are some suggestions for confronting yourself without condemning yourself:

- *Fight fairly:* Do not punch yourself below the belt. Pay attention to your language. Try to avoid talking in absolutes (such as "I always do . . ." or "I will never be able to . . ."). Instead, give yourself a break with language such as "It would be nice if . . ." or "Sometimes I can be . . ."; this subtle change can help you not turn yourself into a punching bag.
- *Do things that keep you humble:* Those are usually the activities that make you reflect on who you are as a person. Try something that makes you learn a new skill. I (Jude) recently picked up golf and realized how negative my self-talk can be sometimes.
- *Don't hide from your issues:* Wear a red rubber band around your wrist as a reminder to stop manipulating people around you.

- *Get counseling:* You do not have to sit in silence facing a mirror alone to confront yourself. Find a counselor and work through some of this stuff.
- *Pay attention to how you feel about others:* One of our mentors believed that if something in another person annoys or upsets you, then it is usually a reflection of an issue you have with yourself. In other words, our feelings toward others can say more about us than them.

## Cohort Conflict

Speaking of finding others annoying, your relationship to your peers is not immune from the stress of graduate school. Sometimes it's those relationships more than the coursework that is the greatest source of stress in graduate school. This stress is perhaps caused by the work it takes to maintain all of these relationships while your identity is in a constant state of flux. Your eyes are opening to your contributions to unhealthy interactions in your relationships. Your cohort members or peers could all be at different stages of their growth. Faculty members are pounding you with assignments. Nevertheless, everyone still has to find a way to work together.

If your program runs on a cohort system like ours did, you may find yourself feeling overwhelmed by the social environment. Fifteen to 30 strangers are crammed into an experience where they are constantly changing, stressed, and comparing themselves to each other. It is a breeding ground for pettiness, judgment, and contempt. This is normal. It may feel like high school drama, but every group goes through different stages as they grow closer to each other. Here are some high-conflict situations to be mindful of while in graduate school:

- *Group class or the group experience:* Some programs require students to take part in a group therapy experience. This consists of the cohort being split into small groups where a licensed clinician leads your small group through processing issues for one semester. Although this experience is intended to give you an opportunity to gain some experiential learning, sometimes the issues discussed are genuine personal issues that your peers face daily. You get to see your peers more closely and vulnerable than ever before. You may also receive feedback that hurts to hear.
- *Group projects:* Whether you hate them or love them, group projects are a part of the graduate school experience. Sometimes these projects are big, semester-long ventures where you

and your group may be asked to do a program evaluation or develop a research project.

- *Differing levels of importance:* We have noticed that some students place different levels of importance on graduate classes than others. In class, we see some students surfing the web or texting, whereas others are diligently taking notes. When the distracted student perceives that he or she missed something important while sending a text and asks a question about it, we see the diligent students roll their eyes.
- *Generational issues:* Conflicts can sometimes arise because cohorts extend across the life span. Some individuals were high school seniors 4 years ago, whereas others are old enough to be those students' grandparents. The cohort develops its own culture, which might clash with the culture of its individual members.
- *Collective thinking:* Collective thinking can manifest itself in the form of a collective idea. Sometimes individual members of a cohort have an image of an ideal counselor in their minds. Like a virus, this image infects others until the majority of the cohort strives to be this ideal counselor. They collectively try to squash individuality (sometimes in a passive–aggressive manner), which hurts. For example, thinking that former Navy Seals who decide to become counselors will never be a Rogerian type of counselor could make those students feel invalidated, like who they are doesn't fit into the profession.

Some students can avoid drama and conflict, whereas other students need and feed off of it. What kind of person are you? We would all like to say we are the kind that avoids drama, but in case you find yourself in conflict with a peer or cohort member, here are some things we suggest:

- *Seek first to understand:* We have all heard the phrase "hurt people hurt people." Try your best to understand your peers' pain. Then respond to their pain instead of however they have chosen to act out that pain in your relationship.
- *Use your resources:* You have some resources at your disposal. You are your first resource. Make an attempt to handle peer conflicts with tact. If your attempts are in vain, then garner support from you adviser. Talk through your conflict with the other student(s) with a faculty present. Your faculty are your second source of support. Process things with them. Make sure

you also own your role in this conflict. One of the key deciding factors in whether or not to bring this conflict to the attention of the faculty is if it reaches a level where you think it is hindering your clinical development.
- *Stay professional:* Professionalism is one of the characteristics you are evaluated on throughout the graduate program. How you handle situations, especially peer conflict, is important. We mention this not to scare you but to remind you that being a counselor is more than a job. You have to integrate it into who you are. How you respond during a conflict with a peer can indicate to faculty how you might respond to conflict in session. Be genuine, have unconditional regard, and show empathy for others no matter what the conflict is about.

## Systemic Issues

Why does graduate school kill so many relationships and marriages? Graduate school can be demanding, especially for nontraditional students who are juggling multiple responsibilities such as parenting, marriage, and working full-time on top of being a graduate student. The stress and uncertainty of graduate school can take an overwhelming toll on relationships. Often the graduate student's partner is not a therapist and may not fully comprehend the changes his or her student partner is going through. These challenges can be heightened when the graduate student's partner is not fully invested in the gamble taken by the graduate student who is chasing a career in the helping profession, which is not one known to make millions. As students get deeper into their program, they learn both how to do counseling and how to be in an authentic therapeutic relationship. Students and their partners might start experiencing what Fuenfhausen and Cashwell (2013) called "spillover stress," which affects the home life. In fact, Fuenfhausen and Cashwell studied factors that affect the marital satisfaction of counseling graduate students. Interestingly enough, they found that stress did not significantly predict the marital satisfaction of their participants; instead attachment styles and dyadic coping accounted for it much more significantly.

You have probably heard of attachment styles in an undergraduate class before so we will avoid getting too technical. In summary, there are three primary attachment styles: secure, avoidant, and anxious. An attachment style develops as a result of an individual's attachment to a primary caregiver. Their style stays fairly consistent into adulthood (Hazan & Shaver, 1987, 1994).

Anxiously attached graduate students have a strong fear of rejection and tend to worry about being abandoned by their partner in times of need. According to Shaver and Mikulincer (2006), a graduate student with this style may overreact to stressors, experience high levels of negative emotionality, and use maladaptive coping behaviors. Often these strategies fail to get individuals what they want—trust that when tough times come their partner will be there to help them cope, hence the term *dyadic coping* (two people helping each other cope). As the anxious individuals perpetuate a cycle of overreaction, fear, and unhealthy coping, their partner's ability to support them decreases. This only confirms their worst fear that their partner will leave. You have probably heard someone with this style say, "I am afraid I am too much to handle." The demands of graduate school are like gasoline to this fiery relationship.

On the other hand, graduate students with an avoidant attachment style struggle to trust others and fear intimacy. Often this is a result of experiencing their primary caregiver as unavailable and unresponsive. A student with this style may not even attempt dyadic coping. They may believe their partner will not support them so why even try, or they do not see the value in relying on someone else to cope.

So, what does this mean for you? Fuenfhausen and Cashwell's (2013) study shows us that unmet needs play a major part in graduate students' marriage satisfaction. Understanding your attachment style may help you understand what you need and some unhealthy ways you attempt to get what you need. This study also debunks the idea that it is the stress of graduate school that is the killer of marriages and relationships. Instead, you should be aware of how you and your partner cope together as a dyad, which has the potential to be more dangerous. If your attachment style is anxious and your partner's is avoidant, how will that influence your ability to meet the demands of graduate school? To us, Fuenfhausen and Cashwell's study provides strong evidence that although one person accepts the diploma, it needs to be a team effort for the relationship to be healthy at the end of graduate school. If you are in a relationship, consider your attachment style and what you need to feel satisfaction in your relationship. Take responsibility for how you go about getting what you need.

In addition to attachment styles and partners' ability to help each other cope, the change process can also drive a wedge between relationships. Imagine that you have been married for about 5 years when you decide to start a graduate program. You and your partner consider your relationship to be solid and you feel confident in its stability. Then you take a marriage and family theories course and realize that although your relationship is stable, it is not healthy. So, you go home that night after class determined to have a discussion with your partner. You bring it up, and your partner sees nothing wrong; your partner does not want to change because he or she is happy. The more knowledge you have about healthy relationships, the more awareness you have about your relationships. You realize that your relationship to your parents is enmeshed. You want to make all of these changes in your relationships, but the other people in those relationships are comfortable in its stability even though it's unhealthy. The wedge grows between you and your partner as well as between you and your parents. We see our students struggle with this pattern often, especially during the first year when the information is fresh. We hear our students say, "It feels like I am growing a ton and my partner is not." Do you stop growing for the sake of your marriage? We cannot answer this question for you. For us, open dialogues and processing of our graduate school experience with our wives and family helped us all integrate the knowledge we acquired in class. ShanTrail King, a recent graduate of the marriage, family, and child counseling program at the University of Mary Hardin-Baylor, shares how her family is a source of her guilt and also her strength.

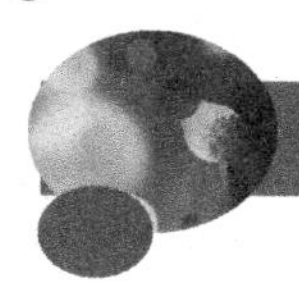

## Voices From the Field 9.1

### Mommy Guilt

***ShanTrail King***

I was so excited to become a new student in the counseling program, yet nervous at the same time. I spoke with my family and received their full support. I registered for my classes, purchased my books, and waited for the semester to begin. Classes finally started, and I was looking forward to the adventure of where this counseling field would take me. As the semester progressed along, my children reminded me of their own schedules and when they needed to be picked up after school. One child said, "Mommy, I have a choir concert," while the other child said she needed to be picked up from her student council meeting. Oh, by the way, I was a mom who decided to take evening classes because I was also working a full-time job. My son would wait up for me after class (which was past his bedtime), so I could help him with his math homework. Have you all seen the math assignments that are given to these children these days? It is utterly ridiculous! Although I love math, I felt like I needed a tutor to help me so that I could help him.

To be honest, by midway through the semester, I was ready to pull my hair out and cry at the same time. I begin asking myself, "What are you doing? What were you thinking? Are you crazy, Shan?" This is where the mommy guilt kicked in. One of the most important questions I asked myself when confronting my guilt was if starting the counseling program was worth the sadness I felt when I was away from my children. Mommy guilt is something that many of us mothers wrestle with. We desire to provide the best for our children, but we don't want our children to suffer in any way because of the decisions that we make.

One may ask, "Why does a mother of five children go back to school to become a counselor?" My response is that my desire is to help people at a greater level. I also believe that it is important to be a positive role model for my children. No matter what life may throw at you, keep moving forward. I found myself apologizing to my children often while in the program. Because of my and my husband's schedule, my children had to miss out on some of the activities that they were in. This really made me feel like a bad mom. The last time that I apologized, my daughter said, "It's okay, mommy. You are doing this so we can have a better future." I almost cried. I came to the realization that we do not pay attention to how much our children look up to us as parents. I had to do what we as counselors teach our clients to do: I had to give myself permission to be in school.

Here are some suggestions that helped me while I was in the program:

- If your children are of age, allow them to help you study by quizzing you. This will help them feel involved in the process.
- Carve time out of your schedule to spend with your children.
- Keep in mind that you are your child's first example in life. Allow this to be your motivation to keep going. If you give up, your children will give up.
- Have a balanced schedule so that you will not burn out. You are no good for your family if you are burnt out.
- Self-care, self-care, and self-care. This is important and must be applied.

The greatest blessing will be walking across the stage obtaining your degree. The even greater blessing is having your children witness you do it!

• • •

ShanTrail King explained how her family helps her cope with the guilt of spending energy on graduate school. The demands of graduate school are particularly hard on parents. ShanTrail King's husband Kenya King, who is also a recent graduate of the marriage, family, and child counseling program at the University of Mary Hardin-Baylor, shares his experience of being a family man in graduate school.

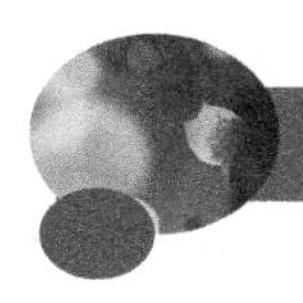

Voices From the Field 9.2

## Family Man in Graduate School

***Kenya King***

Upon entering the counseling program, I felt that I had a very good relationship with my spouse and children. As I progressed in the program, I came to realize that my relationship with my spouse grew exponentially, as did our family dynamics. I gained a better understanding of how to communicate effectively not only with my spouse but also with my children. The life-span course helped me to better understand the cognitive, physical, and psychological development of myself, my spouse, and our children. Although working to obtain my master's degree in counseling did take a lot of time away from my children, it brought me closer to them and to my spouse as she herself was enrolled in the same program. Collectively we learned the many facets of marriage and family therapy, and we applied what we learned to enhance our relationship as husband and wife and our family system. I believe that any person entering a graduate-level program needs to recognize that having a committed relationship, whether it is dating or a marriage, can be quite challenging. You will find that your significant other is often your strength and support when you meet challenges. My wife and I saw each other as "battle buddies." We shared the same mentality, and we constantly motivated, inspired, and pushed each other to complete assignments, work on presentations, and study for examinations.

The three key elements that insured our success in the graduate program were setting goals, having open communication, and doing self-care. Goal setting was instrumental because we both had to work on setting realistic, attainable goals. That meant having to be honest with ourselves and each other about our strengths and weaknesses and working together to reach the set goals. Open communication was equally important. We had to talk to each other to discuss schedules, assignment due dates, feelings of being stress or overwhelmed, and the positive things in our lives. Communication was not just verbal; often it was the nonverbal communication that showed us potential stressors or distractions that affected us in the program. Finally, we have always engaged in self-care, but the idea and execution of self-care in the graduate counseling program was on a much greater level. Although the academic portion of the program was challenging, conducting mock counseling sessions that eventually led to face-to-face counseling sessions in practicum, Internship I, and Internship II challenged us on a physical and emotional level. Self-care was vital for us to be able to maintain a balance between work, school, and our family. Although we got through our program together, we each had our own personal struggles. My wife experienced mommy guilt, and I uncovered hard realities as a man, a father, and a husband.

Life in general forces a man to deal with hard realities, and a master's counseling program is no different. The counseling program at the University of Mary Hardin-Baylor forced me to deal with the hard reality that I had unresolved issues in my own life that needed to be dealt with before I could help others deal with their issues. This opened other doors that I had seemingly shut in my life. One primary area was the inability for me to openly express my emotions and feelings. I found myself thinking and ultimately realizing that it was not fair for me to hold things in when I expected my clients to fully express themselves for me to help them. Another reality was being one of a few men in a predominately female cohort. I was not only a man but also a middle-aged man who was older than most of my cohort and my professors. Initially I felt that I would be behind the learning curve being in class with younger individuals. I wondered if I could retain information, handle the assignments, pass examinations, and also be able to facilitate counseling sessions for my clients. My fear of failure often overshadowed my resiliency to succeed. By casting my fears aside, having a positive outlook, and building on my strengths and resiliency, I lost sight of the things that I thought would hold me back, and I grabbed hold of the things that could help propel me, my career, and my family forward. The hard reality is that I was putting too much on myself. I set unrealistic goals and expectations, tried to cover down on all aspects of my life as if I could not make any mistakes, and didn't give myself any room to breathe and just be a man who wanted to better himself for himself and his family. In a nutshell, I just needed to settle down, be myself, and let things fall into place.

• • •

ShanTrail and Kenya King explained how dyadic coping can strengthen a relationship. They also shared how sometimes letting go and giving yourself permission to follow your dreams or share your emotions can be healing. I (Jude) have had the pleasure of watching both ShanTrail and Kenya King grow into counselors I would entrust with my family. I have seen how they have managed to make their whole family a part of their growth experience. They are embodying community care by reaching out to family members, communicating with each other, and processing their changes as they happen. Their experiences illustrate how personal conflict and relational conflict are strongly tied to each other. Maybe you already see how all conflict has a tie to personal, inner conflict. This is also true in conflict with faculty members.

## Faculty Conflict

Graduate school should be challenging, not traumatizing. We discuss this statement from a multicultural perspective in the next chapter, but in this section, we discuss this statement within the context of faculty conflict. Faculty members have so much power. It would be naive and dangerous for us not to acknowledge it. It would also be dangerous for you not to acknowledge it and accept it. Sometimes this power erodes their better judgment, and they forget why they became counselor educators. This power in the hands of faculty members who are often exhausted, stressed, stretched thin, and facing their own personal and professional issues can cause conflict. Students working with these faculty members while they too are exhausted, anxious, undergoing changes, and struggling personally and professionally does not help. We would be remiss not to acknowledge the power graduate students have as well. Although graduate students need their faculty members' support to obtain their degree, faculty and the university need graduate students to keep the program alive. A program runs the risk of not being a program if it develops a reputation for poor faculty–student relationships.

Embedded within the structure of graduate school are factors that amplify the potential for conflict between faculty and graduate students. The mentorship/advisory relationship can hold conflict. Your adviser guides you through the graduate experience and stays with you afterward. Advisers give career advice and job recommendations, and they can connect you to a community of practitioners in the area for postgraduate licensure supervision. Faculty members are also responsible for deciding clinical placements, stipends, awards, work assignments, and other resources (e.g., recommendation letters, grant writing support) that a student may not be able to use or experience if they are in conflict with their faculty. Another factor is that counselor education faculty are usually small, so your options are limited for a replacement adviser or mentor if you do not form a good working relationship with the one assigned to you.

These factors make it seem inevitable that you will face some kind of conflict with a faculty member before graduation. This is normal, but if you feel mistreated, that does not make it OK. As we said earlier, graduate school is supposed to be challenging, not traumatizing. You have options. The first step is deciding whether or not the conflict you are having with a faculty member is negatively affecting your development. If so, then it is important for you to familiarize yourself with your university's faculty code of conduct and your student handbook. This will outline interactions that are outside the normal limits. Be sure to document interactions and save emails and other digital communication. There are also levels upon which you can seek support. If the conflict cannot be mitigated one-on-one between you and the faculty member, you can involve supervisors, deans, grievance committees, and accreditation and licensure boards.

## Supervisor Conflict

We talked about supervision in earlier chapters, so by now you may get the basic concept of supervision and its purpose. In short, your faculty will meet with you and process cases when you are in practicum and internship. As you can imagine, this process is an extremely personal experience. Your supervisor pushes you to grow personally and professionally. They support you through tough sessions, intense crisis situations, countertransference and triggers, audits or ethics board investigations, and other clinical issues. Conflict is as much a part of supervision as it is a part of therapy. Conflict does not always have to be explosive, and often supervisors attempt to make the conflict constructive. The conflict is embedded in the process because although the supervisory relationship is a supportive one, it is also an evaluative one. Your supervisor is a gatekeeper for the profession. Part of his or her job is to keep the community safe from harmful clinicians. That role makes the supervisor relationship essential to your training. Ramos-Sánchez et al. (2002) found that your training satisfaction is influenced by your relationship to your supervisor.

The supervision process has layers upon layers. The client has a process with their environment, the counselor has a process in session with the client, then the supervisor has a process within the supervision relationship. Parallel processes are bouncing all over the place like free radicals in the counseling and supervision session. Sometimes what is going on in the client's life may also be going on in the counselor's life, and it may also be happening in the supervisor's life. All of these processes influence each other. It is not uncommon for the supervisor's limitation to become both the clinician's and client's limitation. For example, if the supervisor is avoiding some confrontation in his or her life, the clinician may not be able to confront the client, which will then influence the client's ability to confront himself or herself or others in his or her life. It is the ultimate butterfly effect.

With so many processes wrapped inside of each other, miscommunication and differing expectations can occur. It may be difficult for a supervisee to articulate his or her thoughts or concerns in supervision. If you are new to supervision, how do you know what to say and how to say it? What is too much information and what is not enough? As your anxiety goes up in supervision, the strain within the relationship increases. You may also have different expectations for your supervisor. Maybe you want your supervisor to lead the process so that your anxiety decreases. Maybe you actually want to take the lead and get what you need, but the supervisor is not allowing that to occur.

Conflict can happen when supervisee and supervisor expectations do not align. Make a list of the expectations you have for your supervisors and for the supervision process before entering into a supervisory relationship. Developing a proactive approach toward conflict within the supervisory relationship may strengthen the supervision experience and will become especially important after you graduate and start paying for supervision. Regardless of how much it costs, it is your hard-earned money, and the experience has to be worth the sacrifice.

## Closing Thoughts

Conflict is a part of every human relationship. Throughout graduate school, you will undoubtedly have conflictual feelings within yourself. The big question of "Who am I?" lingers over every challenge the program throws at you. As you start to figure out the answer to that question, your partner may wonder, "Who are we?" As you change and grow, those around you may not. Tough decisions and hard conversations may need to happen for relationships to strengthen. This process also applies to faculty and supervision relationships. How you manage these conflicts influences your survival and your ability to thrive in graduate school.

# Multicultural Considerations

There are several things to consider from a multicultural perspective throughout counselor training. For example, to our knowledge, the predominant counseling, supervision, and educational theoretical orientations and philosophies are written from a White, European, male perspective. If you are a person of color or a woman, you may not feel as if there is a theory for you. Additionally, some students have experiences like ours where they were taught these theories and philosophies by predominantly White educators at predominantly White institutions.

We struggled to find a sense of belonging early in our counseling careers, and at times we still feel uncomfortable because of this dynamic. Integrating our own culture into our work was one of our greatest challenges. In addition to this dynamic, unfortunately, we and our colleagues have experienced discrimination and microaggressions from well-intentioned but naive faculty members. Other colleagues face challenges regarding their sexual identity and other cultural issues in addition to ethnicity.

This chapter focuses on our experiences and those of our contributors. We will outline some of the multicultural considerations that students may not be aware they are experiencing in their counseling programs. We will also discuss ways to thrive in a counseling program from a multicultural perspective. We hope the discussions in this chapter will help prepare students to make a more informed choice regarding their education and life after graduation.

## Culture and Graduate School

There is an intertwining dance between culture and graduate school. In our opinion, the culture of any graduate program determines student satisfaction, clinical proficiency, and a healthy counselor identity. Both the student's and the graduate program faculty's awareness of their own cultural values and biases, their willingness to accept the fact that the other's worldviews are different, and their ability to still be healthy and respectful with each other all highlight this intertwining dance between culture and graduate school. A graduate school culture that values connectivity within faculty–student relationships also values and respects the culture of the faculty and students. Connectivity allows for the collective to take part in creating an overall program culture. In the healthiest circumstances, your beliefs, values, background, race, ethnicity, and so on are seen as items that reinforce a culture of connectivity. In a harmful culture, limited connection between faculty and students exist, which makes it hard to solidify a collective culture.

There are several elements that contribute to culture within graduate schools: (a) messages, (b) values, (c) "shoulds," and (d) consistency. The messages that exist within a graduate program are paramount in dictating culture. For example, saying "all students take part in the success of the program" sends a different message than saying "this program will exist with or without you." Hearing that you play an active role in the success of the program may prompt you to take responsibility for your education and the trajectory of the program. On the other hand, hearing that the program will exist without you could make you feel like a faceless student within the program. In addition, the messages can turn into doctrines. Thus, you should carefully consider messages such as "my door is always open" or "we look for potential in all of our students" when trying to understand the culture of a program.

The values that exist within a graduate program are also important regarding culture, and a program's core values can be reflected in the makeup of the faculty. Programs that contain individuals from different backgrounds and ethnicities or ones that contain predominately Christian faculty members are communicating specific values that may be unique to that program. These messages and values contribute to how individuals within the program "should" act. If the culture of the graduate program is more liberal or conservative, for example, a culture of "you should believe, act, or treat others a specific" way may be present. Regarding consistency, the consistent messages, values, and behaviors are what cements the culture. In some programs, the culture is so rigid that students or faculty who enter the culture from the outside can be shunned or blocked from connecting. Dr. Kellie Kirksey, a holistic psychotherapist and certified rehabilitation counselor at the Cleveland Clinic Center for Integrative and Lifestyle Medicine in Lyndhurst, Ohio, shares her experience of how finding a connection with her ancestors supported her counseling program experience.

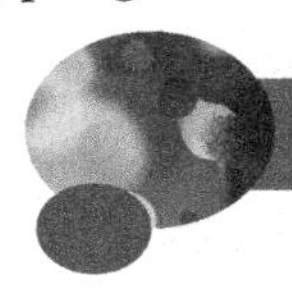

Voices From the Field 10.1

## The Cultural Connection

***Kellie Kirksey***

Remembering the strength and resiliency of my ancestors helped me navigate many challenges in my professional journey. To survive and thrive in graduate school and beyond, I have leaned on those who came before me. I remember the power of their spirit to survive whatever lay ahead of them. Staying connected to one's culture is such a critical point of support, tenacity, and encouragement. As an African American woman, I have consistently drawn strength from those who paved the way for me to be here. It is so important to remember the journey of our mothers and fathers and grandparents and so on. During those moments of deepest despair and doubt in my life, I have used the mantra, "The Middle Passage wasn't easy." This is my anthem to remind myself to keep moving forward on my path in the midst of the messiness of life. If my ancestors, shackled and beaten, had the strength and courage to survive the transatlantic journey to slavery, then I can make it through whatever trivial discomfort I am experiencing. Our history as a people is one of perseverance and struggle. I consciously choose to persevere and thrive.

When in graduate school, I was a member of the Black Graduate and Professional Student Association. Being with other students of color for social activities and fellowship and commiserating with them on the challenges of navigating a system that was not built for us was like living water because this group helped me to survive. Being a member of this group gave me support in a community that could understand part of my struggles because of a powerful shared history.

Community is critical, and during my years in graduate school, I was fortunate enough to have a community that engaged in activities that gave me a healthy outlet and spiritual nourishment. I had a professor who would lead a group of us in drumming, meditation, and cultural discussions. Being in the drum circle, hearing the beat of the drum, and dancing away the tension of life was good medicine. In that circle, we knew that we were safe and supported and could let go of the frustrations and fears of the moment. These practices of my ancestors helped me to return to my sense of being grounded and free. During graduate school, I also began to explore the Native American side of myself. I began going to *inipi* ceremonies (purification lodges) to pray, meditate, and connect to nature in a different way. It was another avenue of nourishing my heart and soul in the midst of trying to balance academic life, family, and health. I needed everything that had been passed down to me to survive and thrive in life.

I continue to use these sacred cultural practices as a holistic psychotherapist. These practices—drumming, dancing, chanting, spirituals, breath work, yoga, and oils—have helped me to survive academia and beyond. I blend it all into my work as a therapist, and I am forever grateful to my ancestors for leaving these modalities for our healing. I often say to clients that if we were in West Africa, we would not be sitting in chairs recounting the history of our trauma; we would be up on our feet shaking the stagnant energy out of our bodies and perhaps a sound or two would rise from our lips and in that movement we would feel lighter, more peaceful, and free. Embracing my cultural practices has been healing for both myself and my patients.

I encourage you to let your culture be an integral part of your academic and professional process. Explore those cultural practices that nourish your soul. Let those cultural practices be a companion on your professional journey and give you support.

• • •

## The Importance of Multicultural Counseling

With the ever-increasing interest in the helping professions as well as the population becoming more diverse, multicultural counseling grows more important. Multicultural counseling deals with how a counselor working with a client from a different cultural group affects the counseling relationship. Multicultural counseling may include dissimilarities in gender, race and ethnicity, sexual orientation, age, religion, spirituality, or even birthplace and family history. Multicultural counseling is important because every single interaction is a cultural interaction. In a clinical setting where individuals are vulnerable, attention to cultural beliefs, values, and behaviors help to capture the essence of the counseling relationship.

One of the most important aspects of multicultural counseling is identifying cultural differences and similarities within the relationship. This should not be limited to the counseling relationship; you can also identify the cultural differences and similarities between you and the graduate program. We are in the habit, especially in counseling training programs, to focus on paying attention to body language, making eye contact, and using open-ended questions to dialogue. The cost of neglecting culture in relationships is potentially pushing people away. Obviously one cannot know every cultural detail or pay attention to every subtle cultural nuance, but it is important to value and consider culture.

## Cultural Competence

The Association for Multicultural Counseling and Development (AMCD) highlights several competencies to achieve in multicultural counseling. The AMCD Multicultural Counseling Competencies (Sue, Arredondo, & McDavis, 1992) is divided into three sections, with specific attention to attitudes and beliefs, knowledge, and skills in every section. In addressing these competencies briefly, we touch on some important aspects of them. The first section of the AMCD Multicultural Counseling Competencies addresses counselors' awareness of their own cultural values and biases. Self-awareness, sensitivity, recognition of limits, and areas of discomfort are noted as important. Also, this section highlights having knowledge of one's own heritage and seeking out additional education on different populations. The second section focuses on the counselors' awareness of the worldview of their clients. Being aware of your own reactions toward other racial and ethnic groups and having an awareness of how race and cultures affect personality formation are also a part of this section. The third section outlines intervention strategies specific to culture. Major parts of this section include respecting clients' beliefs and values regarding religion and spirituality, having an awareness of institutional barriers for minorities, and seeking consultation to treat culturally different clients. Cultural competency is something that we all strive for with the expectation that it is a continuous process throughout the duration of our career. Because the population is becoming more and more diverse, the desire to stay culturally competent is necessary.

## The Role of Self in Multicultural Counseling

Self-reflection is essential in the journey of becoming a culturally competent counselor. This process starts with clearly defining and identifying your own worldview. You will need to consider your race, ethnicity, the messages your family sends, biases, and so on to create clarity. Then explore your beliefs about those who may be different from you and pay specific attention to individuals you may have a strong emotional reaction toward. Explore where this emotional reaction is coming from (perhaps a perceived negative experience with a specific group or messages that were passed down from your family). The point of this exercise is to start a process that will become a consistent part of how you work with other individuals. It is meant to help you uncover your own feelings, prejudices, and stereotypes about clients from other cultures. As mentioned throughout this chapter, continuing to stay open-minded and willing to pursue cultural education is important. It is also important to constantly integrate new learning into your relationships with clients, peers, and colleagues as your career matures.

You can explore the role of the self in multicultural counseling through the lens of the RESPECTFUL model of counseling and development (D'Andrea & Daniels, 2001). The factors within this model influence how we learn to view ourselves and others. It also aids in constructing meaning for the individuals we work with. The 10 factors of this model are as follows:

- *Religious-spiritual identity:* Religion and spiritual identity affect clients' lived experiences in a way that provides strength and ways of coping as well as barriers to resolving unfinished business.
- *Economic class background:* Individuals' economic class can affect not only the services that are available to them but also the way they solve problems and identify strengths and weaknesses.
- *Sexual identity:* Sexual identity can be freeing or extremely oppressive for others. Understanding an individual's sexual identity and your reactions or thoughts is important in our work as counselors. This factor relates to a person's gender identity,

roles, and sexual orientation and has a significant impact on the counseling relationship.

- *Psychological maturity:* Although individuals may share common characteristics (e.g., gender, age, cultural/racial backgrounds), they may appear very different psychologically. Psychological maturity can be determined by an individual's response to situations or the environment.
- *Ethnic–cultural–racial identity:* Individuals can experience within-group differences, which influence their psychological development. Understanding and respecting important differences can help you build rapport and explore deep emotional issues with individuals.
- *Chronological developmental challenges:* These are age-related changes that affect individuals at different points in their lives.
- *Trauma and other threats to one's well-being:* Stressful situations have a complex way of putting individuals at risk of psychological danger. Trauma may exceed an individual's ability to cope in a healthy way and result in psychological issues for the individual.
- *Family history and dynamics:* With the rapid diversification of the population, the traditional picture of "family" is shifting. Being aware of these shifts can help individuals derive personal understanding from their circumstances.
- *Unique physical characteristics:* The possession of unique physical characteristics may cause dissatisfaction for the individuals we help. It is important to reflect on the way in which your own definition of physical beauty may influence the relationship with your clients.
- *Location of residence and language differences:* When we work with individuals who are from different locations than us and who speak languages that are different from our own, it is important to understand the possible biases and insecurities that we may have developed about such individuals as well as the region the individual is from.

Dr. Vanessa Dominguez, a therapist at Whole Journey in Chesapeake, Virginia, and an adjunct professor in the Department of Counseling and Human Services at Old Dominion University, shares her experience of coming out in graduate school and how it influenced her development.

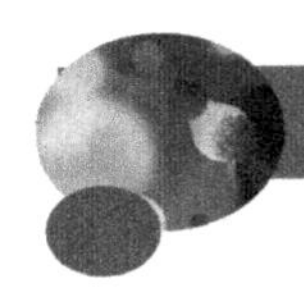

Voices From the Field 10.2

## Coming Out in Graduate School

*Vanessa Dominguez*

Reflection on one's life path is a natural part of life and an expected developmental task of middle adulthood. This examination of life can occur on many different areas, including identity, values, and attitudes. Sexual orientation is an integral part of this identity and affects every stage of an individual's development. I came out in the last year of my doctoral program, while I was in what appeared to be an ideal marriage. During this process, I incurred several layers of intrapersonal and interpersonal challenges that required a systems perspective, particularly considering my Latinx background.

When I truly realized my feelings for women, I felt really confused and frustrated with the emotions and thoughts I was undergoing. I felt distraught and extremely distressed. There were many nights that I would lie in bed looking at my husband while he slept and quietly sob because of what I was going through. So many thoughts would flutter through my mind: "How could this be happening to me?" "How could I question if I want to be with my husband?" and "What happens if I keep ignoring them? Will they ever go away? Or will they get even louder?" I could not understand how I could be experiencing such intense desires to be with a woman and to explore my sexual identity. I held on to my feelings for several months, as I tried to make sense of them. At first, I tried to bury them deep down and remind myself that I was married and I loved my husband. I felt guilt and shame because I was so happy and really enjoyed the life we built. At the same time, I felt like there was a growing disconnect within me. On the outside, I was continuing to project this image of how I always presented to people, but internally, I began to resent myself as I tried to ignore what was bubbling inside. There were parts of me that I denied and did not want to accept. Over the next several months, it felt like I had been unlocking rooms within me that were previously hidden. Much to my chagrin, I realized that I was evolving. This evolution coincided with many positive and negative emotions as well as revelations about myself. I suppose the doors began revealing a path to my authentic self. All of which were tied to my self-worth and born out of a need to bridge the gap between who I felt I was on the inside and who I wanted to present to the world. In hindsight, these changes may have started even before my doctoral program, but my depression, anxiety, and desire to be perfect prevented me from opening up and listening to my voice. For a long time, I defined myself as a people pleaser, or a person who puts his or her needs aside to keep peace or gain approval from others. I always relied on others' perceptions of me to feel reassured that I was heading on the right track, rather than believing in and trusting myself, which often led me to be susceptible to confusion and guilt.

Given the need to please people, I prematurely came out to a few people, which contributed to my intrapersonal challenges. I navigated a gamut of reactions from those who seemed to respond with a need to take action of some sort. Some people felt like I needed to return to my vows or that I required guidance on making such a nuanced decision, whereas others seemed to take my coming out personally (e.g., "Why didn't you come to me sooner? I thought our friendship was closer," "How could you do to this to your husband?"). All of these reactions made me feel further confused, ashamed, and guilty for what I was going through and created a lot more noise in the process. Through all of this, I learned the value of holding the space for someone like myself going through such an ambiguous transition and decision. Although I recognize all of these reactions stemmed from good intentions, they stymied my process and created chaos about my sexual identity. Consequently, it undermined my ability to decide for myself and deflated the confidence I needed to move forward with coming out. It further muddied the water for me, so to speak, because I felt pulled in so many directions and naively wanted people to support and approve my coming out, as if it would boost me even further. What I realized is that I never really needed the support or approval of these people. Instead, I really needed to work on improving the relationship I had with myself and trust that I had the resolve to come out later in life.

From a conceptual standpoint, here are some insights to help a counselor who is working with someone at the time of such turmoil. First of all, there is no road map on coming out. I very much appreciated those who were able to hold the space for me. These people provided validation of my feelings and normalized the multiple perspectives of this process, none of which were more important than the others. By mainly listening and helping me reflect on what I was sharing, they encouraged me to go inward to make further clarifications of what this process meant for me. As a result, I realized that many of my intrapersonal and interpersonal struggles were related to projections of others' frustrations, envy, and judgment onto me since I was destroying an ideal image of a person in an ideal relationship. I concluded that these projections seemed to stem from internalized heteronormativity and possibly internalized homophobia, but I did not register this conclusion at a conscious level because I valued the people who also had strong beliefs on how I should be handling my coming out process. At the end of the day, my husband was the only person I needed to come out to.

In conclusion, from a wellness standpoint, I started to build myself up. I began by setting boundaries in relationships that were draining me and limiting my exposure to additional triggers. I started to focus on meeting my own needs such as prioritizing finishing my degree and the job search process. I also stopped searching for others' input and approval to move forward with coming out and trusted the timing of my own choices and intuition. I prioritized internal reflection, which consisted of regular meditation, journaling, reading others' coming out stories, and going to therapy. I learned to challenge the distorted thoughts I had about heteronormativity and understand the fluidity of sexual and affectional identity. It was helpful for me to identify sources of coping and support that were safe, trustworthy, and unbiased. Ultimately, it was crucial for me to give myself grace, patience, and unconditional love for the person inside that was burgeoning to come out. I recognized that sexual identity development is more of a cyclical process of acceptance and self-compassion. I had to learn how to forgive myself for the mistakes I made in realizing that I was gay later in life and how to accept that I did the best I could to navigate my sexual identity and consider the point of view of everyone who was being affected. Throughout this process, there were several important pieces for me to address with a mental health professional. First, I had to clarify that the need to feel validated and that what I was going through is developmentally expected. I also needed help clarifying my boundaries—what stuff was being projected onto me by others and what was my own to sift through. Moreover, I needed help clarifying what I was not getting from certain relationships such as patience, nonjudgment, objectivity, and respect. Finally, it was helpful for me to reflect on how I could have done things differently to take better care of myself and my relationships, especially because I was finishing my doctorate. Overall, the growth I endured during the doctoral program was a catalyst for the shifts I experienced inside of me. As I grew, I challenged the perceptions I had of myself and questioned my core beliefs. The ability to explore my sexual and affectional orientation required tapping into a resilience and quiet strength that I had not tapped into before.

• • •

## Closing Thoughts

Dr. Dominguez's experience illustrates how important it is to understand who you are within the context of the RESPECTFUL model. Throughout the course of any relationship in graduate school, the RESPECTFUL model can help you increase your understanding, awareness, and connectivity. This model can be a jumping off point to understand others as well as yourself as you develop into a more multiculturally competent counselor.

# Epilogue

Thank you for deciding to purchase this book. We hope that it has prepared you to thrive when you can and survive when you must in graduate school. It is a long journey; 3 years in graduate school feels like 10 years' worth of emotional growth. It is intimidating and anxiety provoking. You should definitely quit if after long consideration and discussions with faculty, you decide that counseling is not for you. But if you decide to stay and you push through the discomfort and the personal stuff holding you back (all the unfinished business with your family of origin and the things that still trigger you), we believe you will not regret it. Here are some key messages that we gleaned from working on this project:

- There will be times in your graduate training when you simply need to survive. It may be a combination of personal and professional issues piling up. But there will also be times when you can thrive. Staying consistently engaged in your process helps you to develop into the best counselor you can be.
- Each year has its own challenges. Some of these challenges you will see coming and others will sneak up and attack you. Prepare yourself in the best way that you can, stay humble, and work hard.
- There is light at the end of the tunnel. You will graduate! Focus less on getting through it and more on who you will be when you finish. The counseling program makes you grow up; it changes you. It is a crucible of self-determination. Try your best not to fight the process even if it's hard to trust it all the time.

- Conflict and setbacks are embedded in the process. They are both growth opportunities. The world needs counselors who can work with all different kinds of people. Understanding your cultural characteristics, your biases, your privilege, and other aspects of yourself will strengthen your ability to understand those elements in others.

Counseling graduate school is unlike any professional experience you will have in your life. An entire faculty is there to support you and push you to be the clinician they know you can be. Honor the sacrifices you and your family have made to get you to this point. Step into your potential. Become the clinicians we would trust to work with our family.

Bray, B. (2019, May 10). One school counselor per 455 students: Nationwide average improves [Online exclusive]. *Counseling Today*. Retrieved from https://ct.counseling.org/2019/05/one-school-counselor-per-455-students-nationwide-average-improves/

Carkhuff, R. R. (1967). Toward a comprehensive model of facilitative interpersonal processes. *Journal of Counseling Psychology, 14,* 67–72. doi:10.1037/h0024222

Corey, G., Muratori, M., Austin, J. T., II, & Austin, J. A. (2018). *Counselor self-care.* Alexandria, VA: American Counseling Association.

Crow, L. D., & Crow, A. (1962). *Child development and adjustment: A study of child psychology.* New York, NY: Macmillan.

D'Andrea, M., & Daniels, J. (2001). RESPECTFUL counseling: An integrative multidimensional model for counselors. In D. B. Pope-Davis & H. L. K. Coleman (Eds.), *The intersection of race, class, and gender in multicultural counseling* (pp. 417–466). Thousand Oaks, CA: Sage.

Fuenfhausen, K. K., & Cashwell, C. S. (2013). Attachment, stress, dyadic coping, and marital satisfaction of counseling graduate students. *The Family Journal, 21,* 364–370. doi:10.1177/1066480713488523

Gehart, D. R., & Tuttle, A. R. (2003). *Theory-based treatment planning for marriage and family therapists: Integrating theory and practice.* Pacific Grove, CA: Brooks/Cole.

Geller, S. M. (2017). *A practical guide to cultivating therapeutic presence.* Washington, DC: American Psychological Association.

Hazan, C., & Shaver, P. R. (1987). Romantic love conceptualized as an attachment process. *Journal of Personality and Social Psychology, 52,* 511–524. doi:10.1037/0022-3514.52.3.511

Hazan, C., & Shaver, P. R. (1994). Attachment as an organizational framework for research on close relationships. *Psychological Inquiry, 5,* 1–22. doi:10.1207/s15327965pli0501_1

Howard, B. (2017, March 14). Weigh the cost, benefits of graduate school. *U.S. News & World Report.* Retrieved from https://www.usnews.com/education/best-graduate-schools/paying/articles/2017-03-14/weigh-the-cost-benefits-of-graduate-school

Lane, J. A. (2015). The imposter phenomenon among emerging adults transitioning into professional life: Developing a grounded theory. *Adultspan Journal, 14,* 114–128. doi:10.1002/adsp.12009

Morrison, M. A., & Lent, R. W. (2018). The working alliance, beliefs about the supervisor, and counseling self-efficacy: Applying the relational efficacy model to counselor supervision. *Journal of Counseling Psychology, 65,* 512–522. doi:10.1037/cou0000267

Ramos-Sánchez, L., Esnil, E., Goodwin, A., Riggs, S., Touster, L. O., Wright, L. K., . . . Rodolfa, E. (2002). Negative supervisory events: Effects on supervision and supervisory alliance. *Professional Psychology: Research and Practice, 33,* 197–202. doi:10.1037/0735-7028.33.2.197

Rønnestad, M. H., & Skovholt, T. M. (2003). The journey of the counselor and therapist: Research findings and perspectives on professional development. *Journal of Career Development, 30,* 5–44. doi:10.1177/089484530303000102

Shaver, P. R., & Mikulincer, M. (2006). Attachment theory, individual psychodynamics, and relationship functioning. In A. L. Vangelisti & D. Perlman (Eds.), *The Cambridge handbook of personal relationships* (pp. 251–267). New York, NY: Cambridge University Press.

Sue, D. W., Arredondo, P., & McDavis, R. J. (1992). Multicultural counseling competencies and standards: A call to the profession. *Journal of Counseling & Development, 70,* 477–486. doi:10.1002/j.1556-6676.1992.tb01642.x

Woodside, M., Oberman, A. H., Cole, K. G., & Carruth, E. K. (2007). Learning to be a counselor: A prepracticum point of view. *Counselor Education and Supervision, 47,* 14–28. doi:10.1002/j.1556-6978.2007.tb00035.x